Guts & Glory

Includes stories of 27
awe-inspiring Indian cricketers

Makarand Waingankar

JAICO PUBLISHING HOUSE

Ahmedabad Bangalore Bhopal Bhubaneswar Chennai
Delhi Hyderabad Kolkata Lucknow Mumbai

Published by Jaico Publishing House
A-2 Jash Chambers, 7-A Sir Phirozshah Mehta Road
Fort, Mumbai - 400 001
jaicopub@jaicobooks.com
www.jaicobooks.com

© Makarand Waingankar

GUTS & GLORY
ISBN 978-81-8495-614-6

First Jaico Impression: 2014
Second Jaico Impression: 2015

No part of this book may be reproduced or utilized in
any form or by any means, electronic or
mechanical including photocopying, recording or by any
information storage and retrieval system,
without permission in writing from the publishers.

Page design and layouts: Special Effects, Mumbai

Printed by

Contents

Foreword	v
Prologue	1
Mansur Ali Khan Pataudi and ML Jaisimha	9
Bishan Singh Bedi, Erapalli Anantharao Srinivas Prasanna and Bhagwat Subramanya Chandrashekhar	27
Ajit Wadekar and Dilip Sardesai	45
Sunil Gavaskar and Gundappa Vishwanath	63
Dilip Vengsarkar and Mohinder Amarnath	81
Kapil Dev and Ravi Shastri	101
Sachin Tendulkar and Virender Sehwag	119
Rahul Dravid and VVS Laxman	137
Mahendra Singh Dhoni and Virat Kohli	157
Sourav Ganguly and Yuvraj Singh	175
Anil Kumble and Harbhajan Singh	197
Shikhar Dhawan, Rohit Sharma and Ravindra Jadeja	215
Acknowledgments	231

Foreword

When Makarand Waingankar asked me to write the foreword for his new book, my first reaction was, why me? He will not divulge his reasons; but I suspect that because I've played with and against many yesteryear champions, and seen many others at close quarters, he has given me the honour to pen a few words.

Guts & Glory... A book like this should be prescribed by every school, college and cricket association, so modern generations can understand how hard each cricketer has strived to achieve his success. Let me doff my hat to these champions, each one of whom set out to put India on a pedestal and has certainly done so with flair.

Makarand has written about cricketing greats, he has watched closely during his long career from a freelance journalist to a hardcore critic. Among these, Pataudi and Jaisimha make a classic pair; they truly enjoyed the game. Tiger Pataudi changed the very face of Indian cricket. I am reminded of my school days when a few of us – Gavaskar, the Amarnath brothers, Solkar and some others who played for India Schools – were led by him in a Moin ud Dowla match at Hyderabad.

Solkar, the bravest of us, asked him, "Sir, how do we address you?"

He smiled and shot back, "Tiger!"

Tiger Pataudi was truly the most charismatic captain that India ever had. (One of the most brilliant illustrations in this book depicts Pataudi's response to an English writer.) His frequent partner Jaisimha had flair, flamboyance and a shrewd cricketing brain to match. Pataudi, and Wadekar too, benefitted immensely from his experience. Also described in this book, Renaissance man Sardesai inspired a whole generation of young cricketers in the early 70s. Indeed, he has been so vividly described that the author might well have been a part of that dressing room!

Comparisons are odious as they say; Gavaskar's technique, Vishwanath's artistry, Vengsarkar's courage and Amarnath's comeback are all part of cricket folklore now. Perhaps, Makarand could also have considered writing about one of my favourite players, Chandu Borde, an outstanding captain who scored almost 100 in each innings against the fastest bowling pair of Hall and Gilchrist and the wily Gibbs and Sobers.

To me, the chapters on our five spin greats are both gripping and enchanting. These players literally brought the cricketing world to its feet. Roy Fredrick's mention of Prasanna, Bedi and Chandrasekhar sending a shiver down his spine is enthralling. Only fast bowlers ever did that, as I well remember! Imagine the three smiling at you, spinning a web around you and applauding each other's success – it was a sight I will never ever forget. Just as the fans erupted when Tendulkar came out to bat, so too, when Chandrasekhar was given the ball by Pataudi, 35,000 Indians rose as one and cheered at Brabourne Stadium! These events are etched in my mind for posterity – Kumble and Harbhajan also revive memories of the spin era.

Many of the stories here are evocative and inspiring. Kapil Dev, one of the greatest cricketers of our time, and his arduous cricketing journey. (Kapil asking for an extra roti to sustain himself makes for a heart-wrenching tale.) Shastri and his progress from a No. 10 batsman to a leading all rounder. And Greg Chappell's quotes on Tendulkar, Ganguly, Dravid, Sehwag and Laxman give you an insight into why these men became legends. The saga of the Kolkata Test is perhaps the greatest win recorded in Test history. Modern cricket history will never find a stronger batting line up than these magnificent five men.

Dhoni's rise to fame from a small town speaks volumes of how firmly cricket has seized the country. And Yuvraj Singh's tryst with destiny to become the best player in the 2011 World Cup is the best summation of *Guts & Glory*. Of the youngest cricketers in this book – only time will tell how Kohli, Sharma, Dhawan and Jadeja carry forward the destiny of Indian cricket.

Here, let me not forget the outstanding caricatures by Austin Coutinho. Having played club level cricket in Mumbai, he knows the pulse of the cricketer. My favourite caricature is of Gavaskar carrying his bed-roll and telling the umpire, "Mind looking after this? I am staying for the night."

All the hard work and the emotions that have gone in writing this book make it a must-read for the modern day cricketer. Many congratulations to Makarand for reviving the glorious past.

– Milind Rege
Former Mumbai Captain

Prologue

Cricket, they say, is a game of glorious uncertainties, but cricket is also a game that, amidst its fanfare, spreads overwhelming joy. In the history of Test cricket, which is over a century long, top players have come and gone, but the game remains the same – a backfoot defence has not changed to forward defence and vice versa. As is the human habit, when a few experienced and renowned heads come together at the state or international level, they are tempted to tinker with rules. Aren't they supposed to exhibit their cricketing mind?

To an ordinary soul, donning whites, these rules do not affect those with a streak of genius. They deal with the changes without voicing their opinion. They use rules to their advantage; that's what is expected of them. Whether a one-ball theory is good or bad for the game, the God of cricket Sachin Tendulkar will never be heard voicing his opinion about it. Perhaps it's below their dignity to read too much into the changes of rules. Their minds are well-trained to tackle such frivolous issues.

However, when they do play the game, what a sight they present to masses! Though India came to be recognized as a world player only after winning the World Cup in 1983 under the captaincy of Kapil Dev, the country produced immense talent and legends before that and has continued to do so ever since.

Try batting a tennis ball with one eye shut and imagine playing the fastest set of bowlers without any protective gear; imagine them hurling the ball with no restrictions on rules, aiming at your head. You will realize that batting out there in the middle, is a different ball game.

Tiger Pataudi did that amazingly with his two-eyed stance, which technically created more loopholes for the bowlers to exploit. Yet he played some breathtaking knocks, toying with bowlers, using his majestic drives. To him, a personal bat made for comfort didn't matter; he could do with any. As Ian Chappell said of Pataudi, every time he came to the crease after an interval, he had a different bat. Many batsmen worry about the design of a bat; they need that to complement their efforts. Why would a genius need help from such a tool?

Then there was this short gentleman, Sunil Gavaskar. At 12, when kids are least bothered about the techniques of the game, Gavaskar was leaving the ball outside the offstump even in gully cricket, frustrating everyone. To all his mates, a game of cricket was fun and they were squeezing in time between school hours and homework. To Gavaskar, however, the batting crease meant everything. Once he got in that area, there was nothing else in the world that he could think of.

The more one talks about another genius, that gem from Karnataka, Gundappa Vishwanath, the more one seeps into nostalgia. He came from nowhere and went somewhere. Oh, not just somewhere, but where he was destined to reach. Vishwanath never used his supple wrists to show off a shiny watch; rather, they came into operation to tackle the velocity or the vicious spin of the ball. To him batting was like a game of chess: more often than not he would outmaneuver the opposing captain's thoughtful moves. Vishwanath was a genius par excellence.

Then there was Jaisimha – all grace and style, attracting more eyeballs from women, who loved him unanimously. For all his naughty and mischievous looks, Jaisimha was a serious cricketer. When he was excluded from the 1967-68 tour of Australia, he didn't react. He was a jolly, good-natured fellow who enjoyed his spirits, but that night he didn't drown himself in drinks. Vishwanath knew that he soon would be in the Indian dressing room. Sure enough he was called to replace Bhagwat Chandrashekhar, who was injured. The management realized that their batting line up had more holes than the five wise men from the selection committee had imagined.

Even with no time for acclimatization before the Brisbane Test, Jaisimha adapted himself wonderfully well to the bounce of Australian pitches and scored 74 in the first inning, and chasing a score to win a game, scored 101. Was he captaincy material? Your guess is as good as mine but in this book, what his contemporaries discuss is threadbare.

Oh, what can you say about the elegant left-hander Ajit Wadekar and the renaissance man Dilip Sardesai – both enigmas of the game. Both played international cricket over a decade and both have made a place in the history of Indian cricket: one for winning against West Indies on their soil and the other when England was humiliated in front of their "we-know-all-critics". While these were a little too much for West Indies and England to digest, they too, much like the rest of the cricketing world, eventually took notice of Indian cricket.

Then there were the gutsy Jimmy Amarnath and Dilip Vengsarkar – both showed gumption when standing up to ferocious bowling. Amarnath gave the impression that the more he was hit, the more determined he became. Vengsarkar mixed guts with glorious strokes because to him, high price on his wicket was all that mattered. Both these gentlemen gave valuable lessons to youngsters in the team on what it takes to overcome challenges.

India is a country of great spinners. They had guile, variations and loop. You ask and they had. Quite a few batsmen were stranded when either Bedi or his teammate Erapalli Prasanna foxed them. They would then rush to each other on the plot and hug, which clearly indicated that there was a plan in place. There was Chandrashekhar, who would with most unpredictable traits, bamboozle the greatest of batsmen. All three however, admit unabashedly, that without the presence of a brilliant set of close-in fielders, who risked their bodies, the duo wouldn't have met with the kind of success that they got.

Kapil Dev and Ravi Shastri have been the two all-rounders. One was a natural athlete and the other used his limitations to his advantage. Kapil Dev's rise to fame was meteoric. A decade before his entry in Indian team, users of the new ball, made one think whether we were making a mockery of fast bowling. An over each from someone who could turn his arm over, after gingerly running ten paces and then bowl at military medium, Chandra and Bedi would bowl with a new ball. Kapil Dev changed that. He was a natural all-rounder.

Ravi Shastri, on the other hand, had the knack of performing when it mattered. A highly underestimated cricketer, he did much more than what was expected of him.

The relatively modern lot of Tendulkar, Dravid, Ganguly, Laxman and Sehwag altogether present a different picture. The game played in the era of Pataudi and Shastri was more of an "if you can't win the game, save the game" phase. When Gavaskar would stay put and save the game, it was a win for the team. At no point did Indians have an effective combination of batsmen and bowlers of international class.

Until India won in West Indies in 1971, no Indian cricket lover had hopes to win. The Tendulkar era from 1990 to 2013 changed the very essence of this approach. They played to win and when winning seemed difficult, they fought tenaciously to save the game. Out of the two decades, for close to 15 years, India had a batting line up of style, grace, technique and aggression. Sehwag added a new dimension to batting while opening the inning. No Indian opener other than Mushtaq Ali batted in a carefree and unorthodox manner as Sehwag did.

It was the master strokes of Sourav Ganguly that steered Sehwag towards being the opening batsman. The latter's quick scoring gave ample time to get the opposition out twice – Dravid at 3, Tendulkar at 4, Ganguly at 5 and Laxman at 6 – the Indian batting line-up was perhaps the best in the world to have attacked the opposition. At times, Test matches looked like an ODI.

When India piled up runs rapidly, Javagal Srinath-Venkatesh Prasad, backed by Kumble and Harbhajan Singh became effective. The Indian pace attack was being taken seriously. After several decades, India found a first class off-spinner in Harbhajan Singh. The surface didn't matter to both Kumble and Harbhajan Singh; they relentlessly attacked the opposition. The fielding showed signs of improvement. Perhaps the entry of a foreign coach John Wright had an influence. He tied loose ends meticulously.

Now with all these stalwarts having bid goodbye or lost form, the Indian team is looking for players who can fill those slots. Tendulkar's isn't a slot; it's a place for praying to a deity. However, cricket being a game, somebody has to bat in that slot. Given any walk of life, nobody is indispensable. How can cricket be an exception?

Hugely talented Rohit Sharma was flirting with talent and destiny until both got him to flourish at Bangalore in the ODI against Australia when he scored 209 in 159 balls to signal his arrival. This was followed by a century on Test debut at the Eden Gardens.

Shikhar Dhawan warmed the bench for a long time but remained patient as his Delhi colleagues Sehwag and Gambhir had settled well in the opening slots. The moment one of them made way, he played an impact knock.

And then came the talented all-rounders Ravindra Jadeja and Salim Durrani. As George Bernard Shaw said "What really flatters a man is that you think him worth flattering". Was that the case with Jadeja? Hopefully he too may be bidding his time like Rohit Sharma.

The reason why I paired cricketers is because they belong to one era. Their styles and grace could be compared. The rules and playing conditions in the 60s and 70s were totally different. There was no limit on the number of bouncers. The West Indian bowlers would aim at your rib cage and no batsman with a weak heart could survive. In fact, most of them perished. There were very few Indian batsmen who stood up to that kind of intimidating attack.

The book presents contemporaries talking about each other's skills. If Pataudi was a brilliant captain to Bedi, Prasanna and Chandrashekhar, there was Wadekar who got you the results. Unlike other sports, captaincy assumes greater importance in cricket. To marshal the team's resources for over five days in a Test match is the captain's job. Both Pataudi and Wadekar did just that and with tact.

India has been the country of spinners. How these great spinners operated is something that has been rarely brought to public view. To contemporary generations, spinners can serve a lesson on their performance those days.

In fact two chapters – Bedi, Prasanna and Chandrashekhar in one and Kumble and Harbhajan Singh in another, present a fascinating study. The trio bowled on uncovered pitches and Kumble-Harbhajan bowled on covered pitches. The comparisons may be odious. However, they will make readers think.

What does one say about Tendulkar who has quit cricket after playing 200 Tests; Rahul Dravid the Wall; Ganguly the Prince of Kolkata; Very Very Special Laxman; and one and only Virender Sehwag. One has to spend time in analyzing their partnerships with one another, which to date, indicates that they trusted the styles of their batting partners.

The chapters and sections on Ganguly-Sehwag, Dravid-Laxman, Ganguly-Yuvraj Singh deal with every aspect of the game and some relevant and lovely anecdotes. Greg Chappell's wonderful analysis of these greats adds value to these chapters.

Every line in this book should inspire the young, budding cricketer. While cricket is all about confidence, it is also about how cleverly one handles situations – good and bad. All chapters in the book have some very interesting and inspirational stories to tell.

This book deals with 27 cricketers whose careers I have followed. The advantage that I have, is that after having covered matches from 1969 up until now for 45 years, I am able to present it to the readers. The two eras have been divided – Pataudi to Kapil Dev and Tendulkar to Rohit Sharma. The interesting anecdotes, some mind-boggling performances that I have had the privilege to watch, and very importantly the contemporaries opining against each other, make the book special.

Mansur Ali Khan Pataudi

ML Jaisimha

Being *khadoos* (stubborn, so to speak) is one thing. But that's not a Nawabi trait, is it? Hyderabad's splendor does not end with the Charminar. The city's regal heritage has been passed to the cricketers, and how! One would struggle to define the element of style in Hyderabadi batsmen. Well, a batsman from the Land of Nizams ought to be a treat to the eyes, that's it.

Perhaps, the young lady, who jumped over a fence to kiss a batsman would have been able to better describe the charm of the Hyderabad school of batsmanship. Debonair Oxford Blue Abbas Ali Baig had only scored a half century against Australia at the Brabourne in 1960. The runs didn't matter, so to speak. What *did,* was the manner in which he scored those runs. Baig had batted beautifully. The flair, style, strokes – it was an exhibition of Nawabi batting.

And then came Mohammed Azharuddin. His unorthodox yet natural style of flicking the ball on either side of the wicket was all class. When South Africa visited India for the very first time, he ruled over one of the quickest bowlers in the game. The flair and authority with which he tackled Allan Donald was exemplary. The Eden Gardens crowd went into a trance.

The Ambassadors of Style

Hyderabadi batsmen have always vowed to make the world look prettier. But every story has a beginning, a genesis. There are some who always find followers. And for aspiring cricketers from Hyderabad, it was mainly the doings of a

Hyderabadi and a Nawab that mattered. The duo showed the cricketing world that the game wasn't just about runs and wickets.

Watching them bat would leave me with just one regret. If only Sir Neville Cardus was around when these artists were plying their trade. The Englishman's words would have delighted us.

People view sport in different ways. To some, it's about winning and losing. To many others, it's about having fun. And to a few others – a rare breed, so to speak. It's about style, panache, flamboyance and class. To them, sport is pleasure, a soothing experience bordering on the divine. Watching the likes of Pataudi and Jaisimha would relieve this ilk of all its tensions. The world would suddenly seem like paradise.

Mansur Ali Khan Pataudi and ML Jaisimha were unique cricketers. Jai, as he was affectionately known, was born and brought up in Hyderabad. That style was in his blood. But Tiger was a little different. In fact, his fondness for crawling on the palace floors as an infant earned him the name 'Tiger'. The family knew it right away: Tiger, like his father Ifthikar Ali Khan Pataudi, was born to play cricket. Tiger wasn't born in Hyderabad. Fed up of the politics in Delhi cricket, he accepted his close friend Jai's invite to turn out for Hyderabad. He fit into the Hyderabad culture seamlessly.

The careers of Abbas Ali Baig and Jaisimha ran parallel from the age of 15. And more importantly, Baig and Pataudi played a lot together, right from their days at Oxford. Baig and Jaisimha played school cricket together

and graduated to the Ranji Trophy level in the same match against Andhra. Baig remembers Jaisimha scored a 90 in that match. And in the next game, against Mysore, Baig scored his maiden century. "Jai's house was a second home to all his teammates, be it from the Ranji side or the South Zone unit. People speak of the style element in the batting of Azhar and Laxman but to me, Jai was as good a proponent of this art as anybody. A wonderful captain, he was a great motivator and analyst of the finer points of the game. I certainly miss him profusely."

Jaisimha: The Leader

One can find many admirers of Jaisimha's leadership. Says Ajit Wadekar, "Not only was Jai part of the team I led on the victorious tour of the West Indies in 1971, but we had also played against each other in the Moin-ud-Dowla Cup. He was a very good student of the game and a perfect team man. He wasn't getting runs during that tour of the West Indies. And I didn't know how to tell him that I couldn't play him anymore. I walked up to his room to convey the news. I said, 'Jai I want to rest you' and he said "Jitya, tell me you are dropping me and I will accept it because I haven't been scoring runs and it's not fair to those who have been scoring.' Jai was of great help to any captain, especially in strategy talk."

Watching Jaisimha bat was an absolute treat. He was one of those painfully rare breed of batsmen who was technically sound and stylish at the same time. What more can one ask from a batsman! Add to that his ability to read the situation and deal with it smartly and you had a real star in your side.

Brilliant in Brisbane

But Jaisimha's brilliance wasn't enough to impress the selectors. They wanted something more or, perhaps, something different. Their idea of talent was evidently very unique. Jai was dropped for the 1967-68 tour of Australia. Where did he lack? No one knows. In other words, no explanations were given. But soon, Chandrashekhar was injured and captain Pataudi realized he needed to strengthen the batting. You see Australian wickets were really bouncy in those days. And they had some deadly bowlers.

Jaisimha was duly summoned. He landed late in the evening and there he was the following morning, playing the Brisbane Test. He responded with a 74-run knock in the first innings and a 101 in the second. The selectors were put in their place.

The Australian media and a few former Test players wondered why Jaisimha wasn't named in the original squad.

Jaisimha played the Aussie quicks so comfortably that it made jaws drop. He wasn't afraid of playing his shots. And remember he played those with some style. In the second innings, India needed 61 to win and when last man Umesh Kulkarni joined him, all seemed lost. But true to his *khadoos* nature, Kulkarni held one end up while Jaisimha played his shots, finding the boundary at will.

Kulkarni remembers that match. "Once I had negotiated the pacers, Jai showed a lot of confidence in me. I told him I wouldn't throw my wicket away. We batted for 90 minutes and added 38 runs. Just before the last ball of the over, I brought to his notice that there was no one at square-leg. I cautioned him not to try and manufacture a shot and send it in that direction. The ball took the leading edge and he was caught at mid-wicket. I think he lost his concentration after scoring 101."

Be that as it may, Jaisimha made one thing pretty clear with that knock: he belonged to the big stage. Nine out of 10 players would have cracked under pressure. And no one would have blamed them for failing after a 16-hour flight and four plastic meals. But Jaisimha was different. He made it count. That's what champions do. They seize the moment. They never look back.

Jaisimha was a passionate sportsman in more ways than one. "Not many know that Jaisimha was a wonderful tennis player as well," says Baig. Jaisimha's interest in golf has been well described by Baig, who calls his mate an "indifferent golfer"!

Tiger, Prince, Genius

Pataudi, on the other hand, was a genius. A lot has been written about his one-eyed stance. In fact, on the same tour where his close friend Jaisimha scored a hundred, Pataudi suffered a hamstring injury on the left leg, but he scored two outstanding knocks of 75 and 85. He couldn't play the first Test because of injury and was well aware of the fact that Australian skipper Bill Lawry wouldn't let him have a runner for the second Test.

However, looking at India's condition in the series, Pataudi realized he didn't have a choice. He had to play. The Indian batsmen looked petrified against the ferocious Australian attack. There was barely anyone who troubled the scorers. In the second Test at Melbourne, India were batting first and struggling when Rusi Surti joined Pataudi in the middle. Surti expected Pataudi to give him a few tips, but all Pataudi did was wink!

Pataudi's injury handicapped him. Surti realized this. Pataudi wasn't able to get on to his front foot. He had to play all those patented front-foot shots on the backfoot. On the big Australian grounds, they decided to deal in singles. They ambled around for a while. But how long could Pataudi be contained? Let's put it this way: how could Pataudi contain his natural instinct? Soon, he unravelled an amazing array of shots. It didn't matter that the gentlemen bowling to him were Graham McKenzie and Neil Hawke.

The effect Pataudi had on those fine pacers can be summed up in a statement made by then Australian Prime Minister Sir Robert Gordon Menzies. "With one good eye and one good leg, if you could hit our fast bowlers all over the place, I shudder to think what you could have done with two good eyes and two good legs."

Pataudi was also compared with Sir Donald Bradman.

Lindsey Hassett, who played under Bradman, said Pataudi's attacking style resembled that of the great man. The funny part was that every time he went out to bat after a break, he would simply pick up the bat nearest to the door of the dressing room. No fuss, you see.

"He was a man of few words, but uttered them at the right moment," says Aunshuman Gaekwad, who made his debut under Pataudi in 1975. "Tiger was from a different league of personalities. His cricketing abilities were astounding. I used to make special efforts to talk to him, but he was a man of few words. He was a Nawab, my Captain and an Oxford Blue. Tiger believed in keeping things simple. He didn't mix or mince words. He was never afraid of calling a spade a spade."

Gaekwad always wanted to ask Tiger something. But he was nervous and rightly so. After the West Indies series, he finally mustered the courage to walk up to his captain. "Tiger, what if you could talk and give us youngsters some tips?" Gaekwad said. Pataudi's response was typically tigerish to say the least. "You have come here to play for India. If you are a batsman, you must know how to get runs. And the bowler must know how to get wickets. If you don't know this, you must go back and learn. Don't waste my time."

Backing Them to the Hilt

Pataudi's unique way of handling young players gave them tremendous confidence. They felt empowered. At the 1974

Kolkata Test against the West Indies, India were struggling when debutant Karsan Ghavri, the new-ball bowler, joined the in-form Gundappa Viswanath in the middle.

In those days, there used to be a rest day between days three and four. Ghavri finished the third day unbeaten. As he was padding up before the start of play on the fourth morning, the BCCI bigwigs advised him not to play his shots so that Viswanath could score runs. As they all dispersed, Pataudi whispered something into Ghavri's ears. The captain told him to play his natural game, the same that earned him a spot in the Indian team.

Till date, Ghavri talks of the magical effect those words had on him. It strengthened him and gave him the courage to face the West Indian pace battery. And the 101 in the company of Viswanath mattered a lot in the ultimate analysis. Of course, India won.

Baig's association with Pataudi dates back to their Oxford days in 1960. "While I was the toast of Oxford in my first year, Tiger took on the mantle immediately after he joined the side. He scored heavily and equalled my record for most runs in a season on the varsity ground. Yes, there was a so-called rivalry between us. We then played together for Hyderabad, South Zone and also for India.

Baig says Pataudi was "reticent except in the company of a select few". He adds that "Tiger's aloofness was wrongly interpreted as arrogance which, in fact, it was not. His contribution to Indian cricket encouraged youngsters. His fielding was electric and there haven't been many like him. I really relished the wonderful times we spent together before."

A 'Change Agent'

In many ways, Pataudi was the 'change agent' Indian cricket needed. He started playing on these shores when it was plagued by dull draws and ultra-defensive batsmen. Not to mention the atrocious fielding standards of the time. In fact, at times, fielders would just refuse to pouch sitters! All in all, watching an Indian unit play the game was an eyesore. Pataudi was like a breath of fresh air. He gave the term fielding a new perspective. In his first series, he lofted English off-spinners at will. The spectators were awe-struck.

When he was chosen for the England series after the eye injury, the renowned journalist Jim Swanton asked Pataudi, "Tiger, tell me honestly, when did you really think you would come back to the game?" Tiger looked him in the eye and said, "Jim, when I read the name of the English players going on the tour of India, I thought this was the best opportunity to stage a comeback and score a hundred". For the record, Pataudi scored a double hundred in the Delhi Test.

Bishan Singh Bedi played a lot of cricket under Pataudi. He is a great admirer of his long-time skipper. "I have said this many a time that Pataudi was the best thing to have happened to Indian cricket. Opinions will always differ, but I am willing to stick my neck out and say that he was India's most daring captain ever. He was also way ahead of his time. He inculcated a sense of Indian-ness in our dressing room."

According to Bedi, parochialism was one of the

characteristics of Indian cricket. "Tiger may have had a thousand flaws, but parochialism was not one of them. And to the spin quartet, he was a mentor par excellence. Had Tiger not lost an eye, he would have achieved a lot more. I don't even want to guess what he would have done! I have seen quite a few of his daring knocks and also his fabulous all-round fielding ability.

Bedi is not alone. Many who played with or against Pataudi have similar tales to share. But there are those who list out his flaws. Seldom did the bowlers have a total to bowl at. Having played and seen top-quality fast bowlers at Oxford and Sussex, the Indian medium pacers were not to Pataudi's liking. He was a bit harsh on them because as an attacking captain he wanted attacking bowlers.

Baig opined that the other remarkable contribution of Pataudi was his decision to introduce spin bowling as a lethal form of attack. True, the quartet of Prasanna, Bedi, Chandra and Venkataraghavan got great support from Pataudi.

Pataudi was the one who introduced the 'leg trap' in Eknath Solkar and Abid Ali. And with Wadekar in the slips, he had his strategy in place. But, somehow, the medium pacers couldn't impress him. He preferred an over each from a non-regular medium pacer and then threw the ball to Chandra who, like former England captain Tony Greig said, was "faster than those who bowled military medium with the new ball."

Pataudi wouldn't let the team's limitations restrict his thinking or strategy. The theory 'A captain is as good as his team' didn't apply in Pataudi's case. His combinations and brave strategies contributed to a whole new Team India. One can confidently say that MS Dhoni is the 21st century version of Pataudi.

Pataudi knew exactly how to handle each bowler. He shared an excellent rapport with them. Even Bedi acknowledges Pataudi's role as a mentor. Prasanna, who toured the West Indies with Pataudi in 1962, can't stop praising his captain. Pataudi's attacking style can be gauged from the manner in which he supported the combination of Chandra, Bedi and Prasanna. Pataudi would convey his strategy to his spinners, instil in them the required confidence and leave them to do their job.

Prasanna is a great admirer of Pataudi. He wrote in his autobiography, "Pataudi was not always an easy man to understand, but his seemingly aloof exterior was a camouflage. Deep down, he was a warm-hearted person. I suppose his breeding put him apart from the men he led. But he was easily approachable. He was also extremely intelligent and expected others to be so. Being mature and willing to consider others so, he allowed himself to be misinterpreted. What I am today is, in a large measure, because of his training. A fine 'ambassador', one was proud to follow him to the ends of the earth."

It would be nothing but foolish to presume that Pataudi wasn't hurt when Vijay Merchant's casting vote resulted in his sacking. As a responsible skipper, Pataudi had ensured the team functioned like a well-oiled machine. And after devoting his life and soul for the betterment of Indian cricket, the last thing he expected was to get the marching orders. He had every right to believe that he was a victim of 'politics'. It was vendetta – and nothing else – that led to his unceremonious fall from grace. It may be recalled that Merchant had lost the captaincy to Pataudi's father, Ifthikar Ali Khan (Nawab of Pataudi Sr) ahead of the 1946 tour of England.

In no way do reports and facts indicate that Pataudi Sr played a role in Merchant not getting the job ahead of that tour. But as luck would have it, Tiger was forced to pay the price for his father's frosty relationship with Merchant. Expectedly, Tiger was very hurt and he refused to make himself available to play for the country after his sacking. And he conveyed his unavailability to the new skipper, Wadekar.

A year later, in 1972, he showed the selectors and the public what they were missing. Turning out for South Zone, he cracked a brilliant hundred against the visiting Englishmen in Bangalore. The knock prompted the wise men to pick him. In 1974, when India fared poorly in England, Wadekar was sacked and Pataudi was named captain. This time, he took up the job on his own terms. "Let me be in charge for the entire series; or else, I am not available," was his diktat. The selectors let Pataudi have his way. For the record, the series proved to be his last.

Pataudi vs Jaisimha: Who Was Better?

With all the praise that Pataudi's contemporaries have showered on him, one question remains unanswered. Why exactly did they prefer Pataudi to Jaisimha? By all accounts,

Jaisimha was one of the best when it came to strategizing, planning and marshalling resources. Jaisimha was, quite clearly, a great manager of men. Simply put, he could read the pulse of a player.

Saad Bin Jung, Pataudi's nephew (he is often seen airing his views on news channels nowadays), scored a brilliant hundred in 1979 against the likes of Malcolm Marshall and Vanburn Holder. He was just 17 then. Jung says Jai knew how to get the best out of an ordinary player which Pataudi, having played county cricket, found difficult to do. And mind you, this is an observation made by a relative of Pataudi. He is probably right is rating Jaisimha over his own uncle.

According to another school of thought, Jaisimha could never unseat Pataudi because their careers ran parallel. When Pataudi (all of 21) returned to India, he had led Oxford and Sussex which had international players. Jaisimha, on the other hand, was a rookie on the West Indies tour of 1962. And when Pataudi took over from Nari Contractor after the gruesome incident involving the fiery Charlie Griffith, he impressed one and all with his approach to the game. And because the careers of Jaisimha and Pataudi ran parallel, there was no way Jaisimha could dethrone him.

Prasanna, who played a lot of cricket under Jaisimha and Pataudi, has this to say, "Tactically, the best captain I have ever played under is Jaisimha. I think even Tiger reckoned he had a lot to learn from Jai. Otherwise, he would not have readily agreed to play under Jaisimha for Hyderabad and South Zone."

That's another quality of a professional sportsperson. You must be willing to learn, imbibe, adapt and adopt all the time. Pataudi knew his association with Jaisimha would only do him good. And he willingly agreed to play under him. Who knows, many of the tactics Pataudi employed during his India days may have had a lot to do with Jaisimha's style.

Jai's assessment of a player's capabilities was supreme. His bowling changes shocked his team, but more often than not, they did the trick. In fact, a better opposition got the best out of Jaisimha.

Prasanna rues Jaisimha's luck because he never led in a Test match. Had he got his chance, many players – including Test captains – wouldn't even have got a chance to play.

Wadekar showed a lot of faith in Jai in his last tour of the West Indies in 1971. And Jai, "forgetting his loyalty to Tiger and other considerations, helped Wadekar in every way. Every tactical move was planned in Jai's room".

Bedi, however, begs to differ. His views are as important, but unlike Prasanna, he didn't play under Jaisimha. "I didn't play a single Test in Australia in 1967-68, and was also very naïve to understand the need to replace Chandrasekhar with a pure batsman! Be that as it may, Jai must surely thank his proximity to Tiger as well as Ghulam Ahmed, our manager. Both Tiger and Ghulam sahib had impeccable credentials and Jai was no mug with the bat either. His first impact on Australian soil was enormous. The local media couldn't figure out why Jai was not named in the original squad. I got to know Jai much later. He was the truest of Hyderabadis – very warm and hospitable, and had an excellent cricketing brain. He hugely helped Wadekar in the 1971 tour of the Windies. But I'm not too sure if he was genuine Test captaincy material."

Like Viswanath and Gavaskar, Jaisimha and Pataudi were strikingly different yet connected with an invisible cord that seemed to reach their souls. While Pataudi got his due thanks to his brilliant cricketing brain, Jaisimha, perhaps, didn't.

Pataudi was stern and honest; Jaisimha was warm. But what really made these men geniuses was the way they played their cricket. Numbers can't convey their contribution to Indian cricket. Nor can they explain the effect their batting had on the masses. After all, cricket is beyond statistics. It's about the way it's played. It's about the beauty of the whole process. Pataudi and Jaisimha are shining examples of the same.

Bishan Singh Bedi

Erapalli Anantharao Srinivas Prasanna

Bhagwat Subramanya Chandrashekhar

Fear of pace is very different from fear of spin. In the former case, it's the fiery speed of the ball that terrifies batsmen and unsettles them. But how on earth does the humble spinner terrorize these willow-wielders? Picture this: the moment a spinner comes on, a batsman takes off his helmet. Is it an expression of relief? Perhaps, yes. But try telling that to the batsmen who've faced the three spin legends of Indian cricket we are going to talk about.

Spin-bowling is an art – it's a combination of guile, trajectory, line, length, turn and bounce. Artists do not scare people. They overwhelm you; they mesmerize you; they even fox you. It's that wonder in their work, which forces people to surrender. With spinners, a subtle variation is all it takes to bamboozle the greatest of batsmen.

Batsmen are tempted to either step out and play breathtaking drives or rock back and employ the cut or the pull. This is an interesting tussle between bat and ball. Nothing can please the eye more than a battle between a quality spinner and a prolific batsman. After all, it's a game of wits.

The Deadly Trio

The three iconic figures of Indian history Bishan Singh Bedi, Erapalli Anantharao Srinivas Prasanna and Bhagwat Subramanya Chandrasekhar presented the cricketing world with one of the most therapeutic tussles in the game's illustrious history. Completing the picturesque scene would be Eknath Solkar or S Abid Ali in the 'leg trap'. These men would seduce batsmen the world over with their illusory art, force them to play a false stroke and nail them.

Bedi and Prasanna could test the very foundation of a batsman. They offered no respite. No, they weren't brash. Nor did they shout and scream. All they did was administer slow poison. There were no shortcuts against these men. Chandra was completely unpredictable and it was erraticism that made him lethal. He was someone who turned his deformity into strength. A series win in England – India's first on the isles – bears testimony to this quality of Chandra.

"I have always thought that a great clockmaker would have been proud to have set Bedi in motion – a mechanism finely balanced, cog rolling silently and hands sweeping in smooth arcs across the face. Yet, it would be wrong to portray him as something less than human – all hardware and no heart – because he bowls with a fiery aggression which belies his gentle and genial nature. His rhythm, too, has only come after countless hours of practising in the nets," wrote former England captain' Tony Lewis in *The Cricketer* (1975).

How about this compliment from Jim Laker? Yes, the England off-spinner who claimed 19 wickets in a Test match against Australia in 1956, said he would want to watch Ray Lindwall, the great Australian fast bowler, and Bedi operating in tandem.

When it came to foxiness, Prasanna would beat even, say, a fox. He loved 'buying' wickets, especially when the pitch offered no help. He would set the field in such a way that the batsman would be lured into playing a risky shot.

He knew very well that an early boundary would do the batsman's confidence a world of good. Alas, this period of success would be short-lived. Prasanna would soon plot the batsman's downfall.

Prasanna had a way with batsmen. The moment he would come on to bowl, the batsman would go into a so-called 'Attack Pras' mode. The reason is simple. Prasanna may have humbled him on several occasions in the past. The batsman would think its payback time. Fair enough. But Prasanna would hold one back and the ball would literally hang in the air before beating the batsman in flight, off the wicket and either crash into the stumps or into the wicketkeeper's gloves for a straightforward stumping opportunity. The battle of wits between Prasanna and Ian Chappell was a spectacle with few possible parallels.

The Bombay Test of 1968 presented us with an eye-soothing duel. It was a visual therapy. No two deliveries were similar, but Chappell stepped out to Prasanna on every other occasion and, in the process, looking way too predictable.

Chappell's propensity to step out only excited Prasanna. It gave him ample time – and opportunity – to try out his angles. But on that day, Chappell was simply brilliant. He was bisecting the field with precision. Skipper MAK Pataudi persisted with Prasanna. And the bowler repaid the faith by having Chappell bowled.

Chandra: The Early Struggle

Chandra was different. At The Oval in 1971 and on many other occasions, Chandra proved that on his day, he could run through any line-up. Even the flattest of pitches seemed like a minefield when Chandra was in operation. All he needed was his right arm to generate speed.

Chandra's story can bring a dead man to life. He was affected by polio at the age of five. His right arm was in a plaster. So severe was the impairment that he couldn't even hold a glass of water. But Chandra loved playing tennis-ball cricket. He could bat, but there was no way he could bowl.

It took him nearly six years before he could raise his affected arm. But he couldn't hold it up for too long. But that's all Chandra wanted: hope. He started bowling with a tennis ball. And whenever the temptation to bowl with a red cricket ball got to him, he'd go to the nets. However, he continued to keep wickets for the school team.

A few years later, Chandra started to bowl extensively in the nets. And his arm was now coming down nicely at a rapid pace. His speed terrified batsmen. Batsmen failed to judge his length and line, especially on matting wickets. It was because the descent of his arm was rapid.

Chandra tried to imitate his hero – the great Aussie leg-spinner Richie Benaud – and his googly would bounce disconcertingly off a length. And his line would be difficult to judge. The nip and pace he got off the pitch was utterly unbelievable. The deliveries sent the stumps on a cart-wheeling trip.

Tales about Chandra's magical arm spread like wildfire. The state selectors set their eyes on him. Thoroughly impressed, they picked him for a match against Kerala. But he hardly bowled in that game. However, he picked up 25 wickets in the three Ranji matches. Chandra was on a high, but he had a long way to go. On his Duleep Trophy debut, he picked up five wickets. And just six months after his initiation into club cricket, Chandra was on the verge of making his Test debut against England at the Brabourne.

Hats off to Chandra. This is what separates the good from the great. Like most of us, Chandra could have chosen to cry over his fate and give up. But he didn't. Instead, he turned his weakness into his biggest strength and toyed with world-class batsmen. More importantly, he was at peace with himself.

Bedi's elevation to Test Cricket was no less dramatic. He was playing for the India Prime Minister's XI against the West Indies in New Delhi and picked up seven wickets with his tantalizing flight. Prasanna took four in the same match. This is what he has to say about Bedi. "Bish was flighting the ball beautifully to the seasoned West Indian batsmen. He had everything in him to play international cricket."

Having lived in Amritsar in an era when there was no television, Bedi first watched a Test match in Kolkata. It also happened to be his maiden Test! He had never even dreamt of playing Test cricket so early in his life. With Bapu Nadkarni and Salim Durani in the side (both players were more useful all-rounders), Bedi didn't stand a chance. He wasn't all that athletic on the field and that made him a "poor fielder".

Ajit Wadekar captained Bedi and also played against him. "I feel Bishan is the second-best bowler I have watched and played against. Vinoo Mankad was up there. Usually, left-handers find it easy to play left-arm spinners, but I hardly scored runs against Bishan. He was a terrific bowler. He was shrewd when it came to assessing the pitch. He was also a great judge of the batsman's strengths and weaknesses. He would literally toy with the opposition. The English had no clue how to tackle him. On the 1971 tour of England, he supported Chandra brilliantly."

To the Aussies, the Prasanna-Bedi combo was like a death threat. The moment one got a wicket, the other would rush to hug him. They would meticulously formulate plans a day before the match. And more often than not, they would succeed. Back in 1972-73, the cricket fraternity in India was excited to watch Dennis Amiss, the renowned England opener. What followed was bizarre. Amiss couldn't even dismiss the half-volleys. He'd become a slave of technique. The more he practised against the fastish left-arm spinner Derek Underwood and the up-and-down stuff of Norman Gifford, the more he found himself in trouble. Bedi was a different bowler altogether.

So what made Bedi so difficult to play? Chandu Borde, a fine batsman, tries to unravel the mystery. "Bishan was a great bowler. Playing for a weakened Delhi team only made him cunning. More often than not, Bedi had less than 200 runs to defend. Mumbai's Padmakar Shivalkar was lucky. He usually had the cushion of a 400-plus total. I've played many spinners, but none like Bedi. He had so many variations up his sleeve. He made batting difficult even on a belter of a wicket. The batsman would prepare himself to play a certain type of stroke, but the ball would suddenly dip and drop and you had to employ a different stroke."

Bedi's skills gave nightmares to the best of batsmen. Like Prasanna, Bedi also loved to 'buy' wickets. Many a time, you would see Bedi applaud the batsman for hitting him out of the park. Next up, Bedi would unleash one of his many variations and make the batsman look like a fool. During his long career, Sunil Gavaskar has played against many a great left-arm spinner like Nadkarni, Durani, Shivalkar, Rajinder Goel and Dilip Doshi. "To me, Bedi and Wasim Akram are the best left-arm bowlers of all time," Gavaskar says.

Hot-headed, Cool Customer

Bedi also captained the country. Those were the days when Indian cricket was mired in controversy. A man of principles, Bedi reacted and was duly backed by his mates. During the so-called 'Friendship Series' against Pakistan in 1978, India needed 23 off 14 balls in the Sahiwal ODI. Viswanath and Gaekwad were at the crease and pacer Sarfraz Nawaz kept bowling bouncer after bouncer. The umpires were unmoved. They were wary of a backlash and simply refused to call wide. An enraged Bedi conceded the game.

Here's more. England fast bowler John Lever reportedly applied Vaseline to the ball during the tour of India in 1976-77. Umpire Judah Reuben, who worked for the Bombay Police, observed a thin strip of the petroleum jelly on the pitch. He slyly collected it. His investigations gave credence to the theory that the Vaseline on Lever's forehead – it prevents sweat from trickling into the eyes – was actually finding its way to the ball. And as a result, the 'shiny' ball was talking. No wonder India's line-up collapsed like a pack of cards in the previous Test. The International Cricket Council (ICC), which was then dominated by officials from England and Australia, dismissed the allegations. And guess what, it was Bedi who paid the price for raising his voice against Lever. He lost out on a county deal with Northamptonshire.

Much before the controversy erupted in 1974, Bedi had apparently told a British TV channel that he hadn't criticized his team members. It was a top BCCI official who had made up his mind and come to the conclusion that Bedi was guilty of indiscipline. The Board honcho then instructed the selectors not to consider Bedi for the first Test against the West Indies in Bangalore. This was nothing but high-handedness on the part of the official. Sift through the pages of history and you'll see the same treatment was meted out to Lala Amarnath. The Maharaja of Vizianagram (Vizzy they used to call him) was, perhaps, the worst man to have led India. A below-average player, he led the side only because he financed the team's tours! It was he who had Amarnath sent back from England in 1936 on grounds of indiscipline.

Those were also the days when the Indian cricket board was never taken seriously. Our players were treated unfairly most of the time. But slowly and steadily, the power center shifted to these shores. Today, the BCCI calls the shots. Yes, N Srinivasan and his mates can be called bullies, but remember the English and the Aussies did the same when they were in power. The truth is they just can't accept the fact that the Indian board calls the shots today. The 'first world' media blatantly criticizes the Board without ever appreciating the good work it does. The BCCI seldom gets credit for the Indian team's phenomenal rise. Having said that, the board must accept blame for the muck surrounding the IPL. It needs to be more transparent in its dealings. It can't afford to lose its credibility.

Bedi was involved in another controversy, this time in the West Indies. Let's call it intimidation. Clive Lloyd was confident of beating India in the Port of Spain Test in 1976. But the visitors chased down a record 404 with six wickets in hand. The series was levelled and Lloyd realized he had to win the last Test in Jamaica.

Having suffered a humiliating 1-5 loss against Australia not long ago, Lloyd would have lost his captaincy had India won. And when openers Gavaskar and Gaekwad handled the fearsome pacers demurely, Lloyd pressed the panic button and asked Michael Holding to bowl round the wicket. Realising that the umpires were allowing the bowlers to dish out such intimidating stuff, Bedi lost his cool and declared the innings closed.

Says Wadekar, "Bish was too opinionated. During The Oval Test in 1971, which we won, I replaced him with Chandra. Believe it or not, he behaved like a cranky old woman. But once Chandra picked up a wicket, Bish was alright! He had his principles and followed them. He liked to 'buy' wickets. At times, the situation demanded tight bowling but he continued to bowl his way."

Chandra was a very different bowler. He played a lot under Wadekar. In the 1972-73 series, he picked up 35 wickets in five Tests. "Bishan was unique in his own brilliant way. With the easiest and the smoothest of actions, he had so many variations in his armoury that regularly foxed some of the greatest batsmen. He was even brilliant with the new ball, just like the great Vinoo Mankad was," Farokh Engineer says.

The former wicketkeeper-batsman goes on to say that any and every aspiring left-arm spinner should emulate Bedi. "Pras, too, had a very uncomplicated and unique style with so many discreet variations. He was as genuine an off-spinner as one could find. His 'floater', which is now called the 'doosra', was bowled with a straight arm. All in all, it was an absolute privilege to have kept wickets for Bishan, Pras and Chandra."

Brijesh Patel played with both Prasanna and Chandra for Karnataka. "Prasanna was competitive even at the nets. He would set his field and then try to get us out. He could do this in matches because he trained so hard at the nets. He had a knack of studying a batsman's strengths and weaknesses. He would set the field and bowl accordingly. Chandra was a rhythm bowler. If he got into rhythm, he would run through the side as we saw him do at The Oval. I have seen him win us games from hopeless positions. He was a match-winner."

Bangalore Boys

Prasanna and Chandra played for the same club – City Cricketers – in Bangalore. Prasanna assesses Chandra very well. "He is a 100 percent team man who wasn't ambitious. He loves his music and solitude."

In 1968, Chandra was sent back from Australia after his ankle began to give him trouble. Things only got worse when he met with a road accident in India. He was crestfallen after he was dropped for the 1971 tour of the West Indies. "Perhaps, the selectors thought that his inability to master left-handers may cost the team a great deal. But Chandra was different in England. He found his rhythm and everyone knows what happened at The Oval. Later, he was virtually unplayable against England at home too. For the first time, I saw both his arms working in tandem. No one could pick his faster one. He had the unique quality of being able to accept success and failure with the same spirit."

Chandra is as modest as ever, "I used to watch Bedi and Prasanna minutely and observed that they had tremendous confidence in their ability. With such confidence, you have more chances of succeeding. In my case, it was a matter of rhythm and that was very important for me. People ask me whether the three of us sat down and formulated plans. The truth is we never did. Bedi and Prasanna were shrewd enough to spot weaknesses in a batsman. And they would corner him. But on my day, I would just run through sides."

Chandra was really fussy about his field placings. His journey through club, state and zonal and international cricket took just four months. "Before I could understand anything, I was wearing the India cap," he says. Tiger Pataudi was his Test captain. He knew Chandra needed a leg slip, a forward short-leg and a fielder to the left of the square-leg umpire. He couldn't really bowl otherwise.

Wadekar, too, set the same field in the 1972-73 series against England where Chandra took 35 wickets in five Tests. Being a shrewd captain, Wadekar would study the batsman. Once, during the 1971 Oval Test, Wadekar replaced Chandra with Bedi. And once Bedi picked up a wicket, he brought Chandra back on. Both got a wicket each in that spell.

Chandra owes a lot of his success to the fielders who complemented his efforts. He was effusive in his praise for close-in fielders, especially Solkar. "His fielding position was a dangerous one. Mind you, there was no protective gear back then. But he never flinched and took some brilliant catches off my bowling."

The trio of Bedi, Prasanna and Chandra represented a magical age in Indian cricket. Had they played together for a decade, India would have surely won more matches. But the selectors were too whimsical.

During the tour of Australia and New Zealand in 1968-69, Prasanna proved he was a world-class bowler. He took 49 wickets in eight Test matches. And when the Australians arrived on these shores, he was again at his very best. However, he suffered a foot injury during the tour of the West Indies and missed a couple of Tests.

However, things took a different turn in England where the new manager, Colonel Hemu Adhikari, called the shots. Srinivas Venkataraghavan had arrived on the scene and he was in the side on account of his tight bowling and brilliant fielding. Prasanna found himself warming the bench. Being the seniormost spinner, he wanted to be spoken to. That never happened. On his part, Wadekar defended the decision, saying the conditions were not suited to Prasanna's style of bowling.

In cricket, the captain should and must have the license to pick his playing XI. Prasanna was Pataudi's go-to man. But every leader has his own bunch of trusted lieutenants. When Wadekar took over, Prasanna fell out of favour. There was nothing personal here. It's just that he didn't fit into Wadekar's scheme of things. Venkat got the nod and maybe close-in fielding was a value-add.

One couldn't expect Chandra to hit form because he was totally unorthodox and unpredictable. Bedi, the youngest of the deadly trio, says, "It was my immense fortune that I was the youngest and latest to join them. As an upstart from Amritsar, I was always overawed by them. They were all miles ahead of me because of their acumen." Bedi thought he was way behind the pecking order, but it didn't bother him. "I knew I wasn't as good as them, but I was happy to be in their shadow."

Bedi calls himself "just a cog in the wheel" before labelling his mates the "real spin docs". "Pras was the wiliest, while Chandra was a natural asset," he says. Bedi was aware of his poor athletic ability. "I used to stand close to the stumps and listen to the 'whrrrrrr' sound as the ball left their hands. It was a bit like the release of a top via a fine rope. The kind of spin they imparted on the cricket ball was just unbelievable. It was a delight to watch the ball revolve in the air before reaching the batsman."

Watching the English, the Aussies and the mighty West Indians, succumb to the crafty wiles of Prasanna and Chandra, was more than what any university could teach

Bedi. Chandra and Bedi were roommates on most tours. Bedi says that humility was Chandra's greatest strength. But considering the kind of selfless praise he has showered on his spinning contemporaries, the very same could be said about Bedi as well.

Bedi washes his hands off any compliment, but it is true that he was as big an asset to the team as Prasanna and Chandra. The three represent a lot more than success. They convey that victory does not lie in strength. Success lies in not following a set pattern, but carving out a niche for yourself. Prasanna, Bedi and Chandra did exactly that.

Playing at a time when batting used to be India's biggest strength, the trio gave a whole new meaning to Indian bowling. Instead of trying to imitate the pace bowlers of the world, they worked on India's indigenous strength. By paying attention to a much-ignored facet of the sport, the three turned the tables on the other cricket-playing nations by improvising on our strength instead of presenting batsmen with a second-rate imitation of their own bowlers.

Bedi, Chandra and Prasanna represent the arrival of an India that was not shy of trying. They declared the arrival of an India which wasn't scared to be original. They combined well against any opposition. And irrespective of the nature of the pitch, they bowled to the captain's plan. More often than not, they succeeded. Their ability to strategize and execute those plans was phenomenal. Blessed with astute brains, they read the situation and responded brilliantly. They are among the greatest legends of Indian cricket.

Ajit Wadekar

Dilip Sardesai

When in Mumbai, don't be surprised if every other boy you meet tells you he wants to play big-ticket cricket. The metropolis owes its cricketing culture to a potent recipe. Want to play for the country? Find a good coach, work hard, pray and lead a disciplined lifestyle.

However, some of India's greatest cricketers did not take this route. They crossed the bridge because they were meant to.

Both Ajit Wadekar and Dilip Sardesai became cricketers by chance. Both were set to lead a 'regular' life before fate had something else in store. In their personal lives, both got married to their sweethearts. And they continue to be happy-go-lucky irrespective of life's ups and downs.

The Fateful Bus Journey

The story of how a grand sum of three rupees played an interesting part in Ajit Wadekar's life is worth knowing. One of India's greatest captains, he was studying to be an engineer. An obedient student of science at Elphinstone College, his life was consumed with academics. Money and time wise, he couldn't afford to play even tennis-ball cricket as he came from a middle-class background.

One fine day, Wadekar bumped into Baloo Gupte, his senior in college, on a bus. Gupte asked Wadekar if he needed some pocket money. If so, he could be the 12th man of their side and get that allowance. Now three rupees was a decent sum in those days and Wadekar was game. India, meanwhile, lost an engineer but found a captain!

A person who seldom found time for tennis-ball cricket on Sundays, Wadekar would go on to become the only player to have been a part of Mumbai's 15 straight Ranji Trophy triumphs (1958-59 to 1972-73). A captain not keen on technology, he formed effective strategies by observing his players and the opposition.

He needed some exemption for attending cricket practice for the college. But the principal of Elphinstone College refused to exempt him from his science practicals. So Wadekar moved to Ruia College because it was closer home. A focused student, he was also notching up centuries at will.

Wadekar's dream had been to study at the prestigious VJTI (Victoria Jubilee Technical Institute) and become an engineer. But he was coming to terms with the fact that this would have to be put on hold. He had a new dream now.

Fate can throw up interesting possibilities. How on earth would you imagine a bus journey to have such an impact on a man's life! Each one of us must expect the unexpected.

The Mumbai school of batsmanship advocated the need for solid technique – precise feet movements, still head, sharp eyes and perfect balance. This was grilled into every youngster's head.

Within a year, Wadekar found himself in the star-studded Mumbai team. The following year, Sardesai made the cut.

In the 1969 Ranji final at the Brabourne Stadium, Mumbai dismissed Bengal for 387 before their openers walked out to bat with 15 minutes left. Bengal pacers

Subroto Guha and newcomer Ramesh Bhatia moved the ball both ways. One over to go and Sardesai was out. So who would be the night-watchman? Unmindful of the tense atmosphere in the dressing room, Wadekar strode into the middle.

First ball: square drive, four. The bowler followed that up with a good bouncer. Hook, four. The following day, Wadekar went on to score 133. "If a regular batsman finds it tough to play out the last few overs before stumps, how can you expect a tail-ender to handle this pressure," he reasons. Simple and precise, that's how he was.

In today's day and age, you will rarely see a regular batsman walk out to face the last few overs before stumps. Most batsmen nowadays are a pampered lot. They want things to fall into place. They prefer batting on belters where the ball comes on nicely and so on. But here was a man who was keen on making a statement. He fought fire with fire.

Many pundits believe Wadekar played international cricket a bit too late. He would bat lower down the order for Mumbai, which had a colossal line-up. Despite that, Wadekar kept churning out scintillating knocks. Once, while batting against the likes of Prasanna and Chandrasekhar at the Central College Ground in Mysore, he scored 127 on a square turner.

Later, he scored 323 against the same team at the Brabourne. Mysore made good use of the wicket and posted 341. The ball was coming nicely on to the bat but, on Day Two, the wicket showed signs of slow turn. The bounce, however, remained intact. With Prasanna and Chandra in the side, Mysore looked formidable. Chandra always relished bowling at the Brabourne pitch because it has bounce. Wadekar and Sardesai, however, had other ideas. Both attacked from the word go. Wadekar was particularly keen on destroying the visitors and he employed the square-cut with ferocity and pulled the short ball with disdain. He read the length well and early, gave himself ample time to get into position and played his shots. And mind you, in those days there were no boundary ropes. The ball had to reach the fence – a good 100 yards away. For the record, Wadekar alone scored 323.

A batsman who walked gingerly to the wicket, Wadekar was fearless. One reason for his delayed entry into the Indian team was his failure against England while playing for the Combined Universities in 1962. That failed outing cost him a few years. Being an upcoming player, the university lad had to perform against the visiting team.

AG Milkha Singh scored a brilliant 75 in the said match and was picked for the Bombay Test. That Singh couldn't make it count is a different story. Wadekar finally made Test debut in 1966, against the West Indies. Though he wasn't impressive in his first Test, he did extremely well in the Calcutta and Madras Tests.

All about Enigma

Mumbai's neighbour Goa also has a fascinating story to tell. The Portuguese brought with them their style of brilliant football, and there was very little scope for cricket to grow. But football wasn't Dilip Sardesai's cup of tea. He was in love with cricket. Blessed with an exceptional technique developed on coir matting, he was advised to shift to Mumbai's Wilson College. Sardesai had arrived, quite literally, and his natural ability amazed college coach Manya Naik.

Sardesai had an enigmatic personality. But he didn't quite play to his potential. He managed to appear in just 30 Tests over a decade. He scored an unbeaten double hundred against New Zealand at the Brabourne in 1965. Mind you, India were made to follow on. However, after setting high standards for himself, Sardesai failed to be consistent on the international circuit.

But, perhaps, there were others factors. While he displayed brilliant craftsmanship in the middle order, he was compelled to open during the 1962 tour of the West Indies. The regular openers were petrified of the West Indian pace attack. And Sardesai was thrown into hostile territory.

Even Pataudi agrees that Sardesai shouldn't have opted to open, but then there weren't any good openers around. There were many who impressed in domestic cricket, but they struggled in international cricket.

Sardesai was a delight to watch. He was technically adept at handling pace as well as spin. His feet movements were precise. His duels with Erapalli Prasanna were absolutely fascinating. Sardesai admitted that only Venkataraghavan could tie him down to the crease.

He was a typical No. 4 batsman who would relentlessly attack bowlers. At a time when specialist openers were failing frequently, he was impressive while facing the new ball.

The selectors asked him to open against the New Zealand attack of Bruce Taylor and Dick Motz in 1965 after he had done exceedingly well in the 1963-64 series against England batting in the middle order and later against Australia in 1964 when he scored an impressive half-century as an opener. Taylor and Motz weren't easy to tackle, but Sardesai paced his innings so well that he scored an unbeaten double hundred followed by another hundred in the next Test.

The move to make Sardesai open was hailed by everyone and the selectors were praised. He too was happy because he didn't have to compete with M.A.K. Pataudi, Chandu Borde and Hanumant Singh in the middle order. What no one could see was that the batsman who relished playing strokes was curbing his style, becoming inhibited.

Role Reversal

The role reversal put him under tremendous pressure. What followed was a string of failures and Sardesai was dropped. The selectors did not take responsibility. Fortunately for him, captain Ajit Wadekar was given an option by the selection committee to choose between Borde and Sardesai for the 1971 West Indies tour and he preferred Sardesai.

Sardesai was brilliant in the middle order. His career was on the right track until 1966-67. A batsman of the classical mould, he relished stepping out to spinners. Now, he was stuck at the crease. He didn't look the Sardesai of old. Those delectable cuts and classy drives disappeared.

Would he fade away? In 1970-71, he got picked for the tour of the West Indies. Borde or Sardesai? Having played a lot with the latter, Wadekar knew whom to pick. This move turned out to be a masterstroke and how!

The Renaissance Man

India's batsmen failed on several occasions on that tour. Only Sardesai and youngsters Gavaskar and Solkar looked the part. Sardesai turned out to be the Renaissance man of Indian cricket. But for him, India would have found it difficult to win the series.

Says Gavaskar, "Sardesai was one of the finest technicians in Indian cricket. He was super-confident too and it was that confidence that gave all of us the belief that we could tackle and beat the West Indies in 1971."

Captaincy Drama

Sardesai never looked like captaincy material. But by picking him to be part of the team, Wadekar proved himself as an able man for the job. And once he led the team to victory in England, even his detractors had to admit that though he wasn't as charismatic as Pataudi, he could utilize the resources made available to him in an efficient manner. And yes, he was a shrewd captain.

How Wadekar got the captaincy is an interesting story

in itself. One afternoon, while he was out buying curtains for his house, Vijay Merchant and his colleagues in the selection committee were holding an intense discussion. It was to be a toss-up between Pataudi and Wadekar for captain.

Of the five selectors, East Zone's M.N. Dutta Roy was absent – mysteriously one may add – and the house was divided on the issue. Then believe it or not, the four wise men decided to go in for a vote. It was 2-2 and that's when Merchant (representing the West Zone) chose to play his trump card.

Merchant exercised his casting vote: Pataudi was sacked.

This remains the most controversial act by any selection committee chairman in the history of Indian cricket. In fact, no chief selector had done till then, or ever since, a Merchant!

Incidentally, of the five, only South Zone's CD Gopinath is alive. Central Zone's MM Jagdale (his son Sanjay has served Indian cricket as a selector and BCCI secretary) and North Zone's Bal Dani were the others on that panel.

Pataudi, one understands, had the support of Jagdale and Gopinath. Merchant and Dani were in favour of Wadekar. Had he been present, Dutta Roy would have voted for Pataudi, preventing Merchant from scripting a dubious chapter.

Wadekar, of course, had no inkling that he was to replace Pataudi. His shopping exercise therefore, continued for a couple of hours.

"Pataudi took the selectors' decision in his stride. When

I asked him if he was willing to play under me, he promptly said 'yes'. As for me, I assured Pataudi he would be in my side, which was to be picked the next day. In the morning, though, Pataudi rang me up and said he was opting out for personal reasons. He wished me good luck and added I should convey his non-availability to the selectors. I was disappointed, but there was nothing I could do," Wadekar recalls.

Wadekar acknowledges that he hadn't scored as prolifically in the Ranji Trophy as he used to. By the way, Team India had no international commitments after the 1969-70 home series against Bill Lawry's Australia. And in fact, he had jokingly requested Pataudi to ensure he wouldn't be dropped!

"That was when both of us happened to be together at the Brabourne nets. And as it happened, Pataudi was unceremoniously sacked and I was suddenly in the hot seat," Wadekar says. "Whatever anybody may say, Pataudi and I had a good understanding and we often had a drink together. Often, he would consult me. And when he played under my captaincy (the 1972-73 series versus Tony Lewis's England), I didn't hesitate to walk up to him and seek help and advice. I regard Pataudi as one of the finest captains the game of cricket has ever had."

Wadekar remains in the dark over why Merchant chose him over Pataudi, but rumour has it that the chairman's "strained" relationship with Pataudi's father (Iftikhar Ali Khan, who played for England and India) influenced the casting vote move. To settle an old score, Merchant 'punished' his adversary's son.

As has been well documented, Wadekar created history in the West Indies and, a few months later, also beat England in England. In 1974-75, however, Pataudi was back as captain after Wadekar's (premature) retirement.

Superstitions Are Good

Wadekar was extremely superstitious, and his beliefs have given us many hilarious anecdotes. Once, Wadekar locked up Gavaskar in the toilet.

During a Test match, Gary Sobers was not clicking with the bat. Besides that, he had dropped Gavaskar a couple of times in the slips too. All this happened during the first two Tests. During one of his regular visits to the Indian dressing room during the third Test, he grazed past Gavaskar's shoulder. Back on the field, his next knock was a century. He did the same in the next couple of Tests.

On the fourth day, Sobers was off the field because of an injury. India were yet to bat on the last day of the Test, but news came in that Sobers was fit and on his way out for a morning walk. When Wadekar realized that Sobers was walking towards the Indian dressing room, he wasted no time in locking up Gavaskar in the restroom. Says Gavaskar, "Wadekar made sure I stayed inside the bathroom till Sobers left the room." Gavaskar had remained not-out overnight but the skipper had to hide him. For the record, Sobers was bowled first ball."

Wadekar's 'trick' worked! That he actually locked Gavaskar in the toilet was extraordinarily funny.

Former Mumbai captain Milind Rege says, "When I was 18, I came face-to-face with Pataudi, M.L. Jaisimha, Borde and Hanumant Singh. Wadekar put his arm around me and said, "You are playing for Mumbai. You should not bother about whoever is batting in front of you. Just bowl well." Wadekar knew how to encourage his bowlers.

A Love Affair Like No Other

Sardesai by nature was a serious cricketer. To him cricket was a religion. He would practice diligently and pay the minutest attention to the technique of batting. A boy from 'Sushegat' Goa, he had come down to Mumbai to make a career in cricket. Later, after retiring, he spent time watching matches in the maidans of Mumbai. Hunting for talent was his hobby. He would spot a boy and then tell the friends, hey that boy looks good in batting but he is a 'chuckoo' (extra smart). He would then keep an eye on his performances. He didn't like cricketers having girlfriends and taking them for movie. No cricketers wear glares even playing for Mumbai. For a person who hated all the nonsensical stuff, which he thought would interfere with cricket, his love story is hilarious.

Berry's Restaurant (Churchgate) was where Nandini and Dilip first met. Nandini had just finished her final exams and was in Bombay on a holiday. They met again when Dilip played an inter-university match in Ahmedabad. The ground was right next to her school. Two months later, Dilip was in Baroda for a Ranji Trophy game.

Nandini was a student at the MS University there. Soon, they were in love.

The Indian team was in the Caribbean playing the all-important series of 1962. Sardesai was there. His job was to tackle the lethal West Indian attack. But he wasn't able to focus on the job at hand. Sardesai's heart was in Baroda, where a 17-year-old was waiting for him. The lovebirds wrote to each other every day.

Nandini Pant was a trifle worried about her parents finding out about the affair. She persuaded a clerk in the post office to hand over the letters directly to her. The clerk agreed to help. By the end of India's three-month-long tour to the Caribbean, Dilip and Nandini had written 90 letters to each other!

"Half of my love letters used to be spent in correcting Dilip's English, but that love was very much there. The teacher in me was born then," Nandini says. When she gave her BA final exam in Mumbai, Dilip waited outside the examination hall every single day with a flask of coffee.

Besides being a hardcore romantic, Sardesai was also a light-hearted prankster. All-rounder Salim Durani was his roommate in those days. One evening, Durani received a call from someone who spoke like a West Indian. The man, who identified himself as an Indian settled in the West Indies, wanted to meet Mr Durani at the reception.

Durani went downstairs, but saw no one. He came back to his room, changed into his pajamas and then the phone rang again. "We want to present you with a camera and a TV," the caller said, adding he was "near the swimming pool". Salim went downstairs yet again and found no one at the swimming pool. Annoyed and frustrated, he felt a pat on the back. Sardesai was the culprit. Durani holds Sardesai in high esteem and often recalls those great Rajasthan-Bombay encounters.

Sardesai was also into neologism. While Wadekar kept his dictionary thin and simple, Dilip thought new words were needed to describe the world. He came up the term 'popatwadi' to address a useless player, or team. During the 1971 series in the West Indies, he saw off the first few overs before screaming, "This is a popatwadi attack." And he sure exploited the popatwadi bowling to the fullest and proved that it was indeed, well, popatwadi. He scored 642 runs in four Tests.

After his showing on the twin tours of the West Indies and England, Sardesai was expected to shine on the slow and low subcontinental pitches as well. England, led by Tony Lewis, was in India for a series. The first Test was in Delhi and the pitch was fresh in the morning. The England batsmen made complete use of the conditions and demolished the Indians. Sardesai, too, fell cheaply.

Months earlier, India had beaten England in their own backyard. And understandably, Indian fans were hopeful of a similar result on these shores. Hence, there was a lot of hue and cry when India lost the series. Heads rolled and even though Sardesai remained in the team, he no longer fitted into Wadekar's scheme of things. That was the end of his international cricketer.

Wadekar, too, was a victim of the emotional outburst of India's cricket lovers. Having tasted success, fans expected their team to win every series. This was heightened after England were almost beaten in India.

Barring a few changes, the same team went for the first half of the English summer. The biting cold meant our bowlers couldn't grip the ball. Pitches were conducive to seam bowling.

The Downfall

At Lord's, India were bowled out for a paltry 42! That was enough for the fans to lose their cool. Wadekar, who till recently had been the darling of the masses, faced the wrath of thousands. His house was stoned by the very people who had once thronged the airport to welcome the team with garlands.

Crowd hysteria is one thing. But what does one do when the administration gets influenced by the public? The worst was yet to come. The West Zone selectors threatened to drop Wadekar if he didn't quit. This was unheard of in Indian cricket.

Wadekar had no option but to announce his retirement from first-class cricket. And he had no one to blame. The very fans who had given him demi-god status forced him to call it a day. Wadekar's popularity cost him his career.

Wadekar's career had started with a stroke of luck and ended with the same. It was bad luck this time. He played no role in initiating his career or ending it. Sardesai, too, was a victim of the mob frenzy. Ironically, it was Wadekar who had to drop Sardesai because of the fans' pressure. Little did Wadekar know that he'd meet the same fate in a few months' time. But it was Wadekar who had picked Sardesai over Borde for the epic West Indies tour. The lives of these players were mastered by large, overarching strokes of fate.

Fate gave them their highs and fate gave them their lows. But both continued to live life full-heartedly and without grudges. Wadekar and Sardesai continue to be the benchmark for Mumbai's *gharana* of solid batting.

Sunil Gavaskar

Gundappa Vishwanath

The gullies of Mumbai have produced many a champion cricketer. Decades ago, a lad from Chikhalwadi in south Mumbai took to the game he so passionately loved. His father had played club cricket and fared pretty well. His mama (maternal uncle) was a Test player. Later, he served as a national selector. The little boy looked up to the elders in the family. Quite literally! Short as he was, he knew he had a long way to go. The journey wasn't to be too easy. And it wasn't.

A few thousand miles away from Mumbai, another youngster was also keen on playing the game. He didn't have a cricketer uncle or father, yet he was madly in love with the sport. When he attended a selection trial at school, the man in charge told him rather bluntly that he was way too short.

These little boys were as different as chalk and cheese. However, they carried the burden of the Indian team together on their shoulders, for a number of years. They were diminutive, but their spirited nature enabled them to scale many a mountain peak. They were little men with big aspirations.

Sunil Gavaskar and Gundappa Vishwanath are of the same height but even today, Gavaskar claims he stands a few centimetres taller. It is difficult to comprehend how differently two greats of the same height could think about the game. Gavaskar was very old-school, much like the manager of a nationalized bank. Safety was his watchword. Vishy, on the other hand, lived life on the edge. He would give it all. Ah, and those breathtaking strokes of his! It was pure joy.

The dynamics of the Sunny-Vishy combine is a favourite of many a follower of Indian cricket. It was a deadly combination. A lot has been said and written about this. But it needs to be analyzed differently. Did they bat according to their mental make-up and natural tendency? Or did they condition and train themselves to do what they did? Why did Gavaskar decide to take the attack route only towards the fag end of his career? Why not earlier? What prompted him to alter his approach in his sunset days?

The willow resembled a violin in Vishy's hands. The man was an unpolished diamond. Born in Bhadrawati and raised in Bangalore, he shone like a gem. The connoisseurs of the game have had different questions.

The ones stationed in the air-conditioned rooms of the pavilion or for that matter, the press box, might have a different perspective. But the ones sitting in the roofless East Stand, which bears the brunt of the sun, admired their batsmanship without probing his technique.

All they wanted to know was why Gavaskar didn't display his repertoire of shots from day one. He would have surely scored at least 5,000 more runs that way and done full justice to his talent. Similarly, they ask of Viswanath's compulsive desire to bisect the field every now and then. Had he restricted his strokeplay a little, would he not have scored more centuries? These questions have no answers. Cricket is not a game of ifs and buts.

Vishy ruled when he batted. The analogy was simple: Viswanath scores a century and India would win. Differently put, India would have won more Test matches had Vishy scored more centuries.

Some questions don't have answers but to be fair to Gavaskar, he was overburdened as an opener. He couldn't have indulged in carefree strokeplay as the rest of the batsmen were way too brittle. They just couldn't handle the fast bowlers of yore. SMG was the sheet anchor of the team. The team needed every ounce of his steadfastness. With there being no restrictions on the number of bouncers, every bowler attacked him with ferocity. And once they got him, the game was as good as over.

Chetan Chauhan was Gavaskar's opening partner for many years. "I played a lot with and against Sunil before we opened in Tests. Even with his aggressive mental make-up, he always put the team's interest before anything else," Chauhan, a Delhiite, says.

Chauhan remembers an occasion – one and only, so to speak, when Gavaskar got really annoyed. The year was 1979. The British press was having a go at him and the Indian team. India was faring badly as a team. "At The Oval in London, Sunil told me that come what may, we must save this Test." In fact, India almost won that Test. Chauhan and Gavaskar shared a 213-run stand. "Frankly speaking, I, too, was very annoyed because the criticism was unwarranted." In that Test, Gavaskar was determined to set the record straight. He played some breathtaking shots, dancing down the wicket against spinners and all. For the record, he scored 221.

The other partnership Chauhan cherishes came against Pakistan in Faisalabad in 1978. "That was a great knock by Sunil. An India-Pakistan match was always a stressful game and we were playing them after a gap of 17 years. Though it was supposed to be a 'Friendship Series', the intensity was quite high. But Sunil kept his cool. We complimented each other well."

Viswanath's case was different. The more the pressure, the better he would play. He is remembered for some brilliant knocks, one of them an unbeaten 97 against the West Indies in Chennai in 1979. On a bouncy Chepauk pitch, the quicks were pitching it short. The ball was flying all over the place, looking for blood.

When Bishan Singh Bedi walked in to bat, the scoreboard read 117/8. The end was in sight, but Vishy was in the zone. He generally was in such situations. Let's say he put the foot on an imaginary accelerator. All of a sudden, he began to hit the Caribbean bowlers all over the park. And who were they? Andy Roberts, Keith Boyce and Bernard Juilen! What a sight it was! Vishy was involved in a 52-run stand with Bedi and a further 21 with last man BS Chandrasekhar. India's total of 190 was a decent score. More than enough, actually. India won the Test by 100 runs.

There were those powerful cuts played with disdain and those majestic back-foot drives. Vishy was bisecting the field at will – the classy flick of the wrist brought on display an array of sweetly-timed shots. Vishy's tactics had rattled the fast bowlers. All they could think of dishing out the short stuff. Beside the point fielder was a sweeper cover. There was also a man at deep point. These positions were unheard of at the time. It was almost like Vishy's batting made the West Indians invent these positions! And yet Vishy shred the attack to pieces.

Calling himself an unadulterated fan of Vishy, Bedi

says, "Gundappa Vishwanath was the champion batsman of our times, and I'd like to cherish that memory till my last breath. Vishy was the ultimate artist, never cut out for statistics. Had he been conscious of numbers, Vishy would have been drab, like many we are all familiar with. His 97 not out at Chepauk was worth many double or triple tons." Vishy, Bedi adds, was a team man to the core. He entertained his colleagues with his unique sense of humour all the time.

Gavaskar was brought up in the cricket-mad city of Mumbai. And he was guided by his father and maternal uncle. But Viswanath had no such pedigree. Neither did he have the support of a passionate city nor elders to assist him. Like any enthusiastic kid, he played tennis-ball cricket without any formal guidance.

When Vishy attended the state junior selection trials, the selectors found him a little too short. It was easy to ignore his physique, but there was no way you couldn't notice his talent. In a club match played on a matting wicket, he whacked the main opposition bowler all over the park and impressed the captain of Mysore, V Subramanya. Vishy was immediately invited to train with the Ranji Trophy team.

Soon, Vishy next found himself making his Ranji Trophy debut. Two down for none, Mysore were in tatters. Vishy batted like only he could. He smashed an unbeaten 230 against Andhra at Vijaywada in 1967. Gundappa Vishwanath had arrived.

In his very first Test innings against Australia in Kanpur, Viswanath was out for a duck. "In the second innings, I was padded up and very nervous. My confidence was shattered. Our captain, Tiger Pataudi, patted me on the shoulder and said, "Relax. I know your ability. You will get a hundred in this innings." The effect those words had on Vishy's psyche can't be explained in words. It was surreal. "Seeing the faith the captain had in me, I got a feeling that I could achieve anything. And badly wanted to live up to his expectations," Vishy says.

He duly scored a century in the second innings of his maiden Test.

"My philosophy was simple. International fast bowlers would obviously not give away length balls so that you can happily play the drive. They used to bang it in short or bowl short of a length. I decided to have one power shot to deal with all of this: the square cut. I practised it every day for hours together. I know I got out a few times playing that shot, but it brought me plenty of runs," Vishy explains.

Viswanath had announced himself on the big stage and it was obvious that he was here to stay. Looking at him play, one wondered what sort of a plan he would chalk out prior to the start of the match. Did he even have a plan?

Gavaskar was, of course, a staunch believer of the maxim, 'Stay at the wicket and the runs will eventually come'. He seldom looked at the scoreboard.

Viswanath was completely different. He always gave the impression that he was out to enjoy himself. Perhaps, too many thought processes would have curbed his natural style of batting. Aunshuman Gaekwad is spot-on when he says that Vishy never planned his innings. It was knock that automatically planned itself when Vishy played.

Opening with Gavaskar was a totally different experience for Gaekwad. "Sunil used to plan his innings very well. He never used to waste time to pick the ones and twos till he settled in. He was cautious with good bowlers and made up for it cashing in on the ones who weren't so great," he says.

It wasn't that Gavaskar didn't like to score runs. He wasn't 'greedy'. He waited for his time. He took the bowlers on when he thought he should; there was no hurry. "He was confident of his abilities and planned his innings accordingly. His concentration, determination and precise technique left the bowlers tired. He would know exactly who the tired bowlers and fielders were. And he would then launch an attack. Most of his runs would thereon."

On the other hand, there was Viswanath! Bedi doubts if he ever looked at the ball while cutting it late. "He gave me the impression he looked towards extra-cover while playing the cut!" Bedi is referring to that match against the West Indies in Chennai where he and Vishy shared a famous partnership.

Gavaskar and Viswanath were as different as apples and oranges. And yet, they belonged to the same basket – the same golden era of cricket. The difference in their attitude could be accredited to the roles they had to play. Sunil opened the batting and Vishy played at No. 4.

Without taking any credit away from Vishy or any of the others in the team, it must be mentioned here that Gavaskar's was the prized wicket in the Indian batting line-up. He was the base of the house of the cards. The opposition knew that getting him would mean half the

job done. They knew that once he was gone, they could relentlessly attack the others. And with a rather long tail, the Indians would fold up. More often than not, this is what happened.

In an era where there was no limit on the number of bouncers a bowler could bowl or the presence of neutral umpires, Gavaskar had to bear the brunt of unfair and aggressive tactics of the opposition. He had to make sure he stood his ground and fought them tooth for tooth. It's not that Gavaskar didn't have the strokes. Once in a while, he would offer a glimpse into the 'other' side of his batting repertoire. He did it while scoring his 29th Test hundred against the West Indies in New Delhi. He went on hooking Michael Holding, Malcolm Marshall and the others at will. It was his fastest Test hundred. Gavaskar could play freely if he liked. Nay, if he wanted to. But he chose to play the role of the sheet anchor. He would block one end up and concentrate on exhausting the bowlers. That way, he made the job of the rest of the batsmen quite easy.

Vishy didn't believe that holding himself up was worth it. In the 1975 Kolkata Test against the West Indies, India was three down for 36. A nervous Gaekwad was making his debut in front of the huge Eden Gardens crowd. When Gaekwad reached the middle all tense and worried, Vishy walked up to him all smiles. "Be watchful, but don't worry. I am there." These words relaxed Gaekwad and the duo produced a match-winning partnership of 129 runs.

When it came to chasing huge targets, Gavaskar carried out the task with a completely different frame of mind.

The ever-famous chase of 404 against the West Indies in Trinidad in 1976 was construed by Gavaskar. And he did it with utmost care. The very thought of chasing 404 made the others nervous. Gavaskar wanted to break the task into smaller tasks. He took it session by session. Slowly but steadily, India got there. And they rewrote history.

When Mohinder Amarnath joined Gavaskar in the middle, they started stealing singles. The field was spread out. It was only when the Indians had reached 200/2 that skipper Clive Lloyd realized what the visiting batsmen were doing. By then Gavaskar, who had raised his hundred, had built a solid base for a counter-attack. And finally, with the two stroke players, Viswanath and Brijesh Patel, in attack mode, the West Indies succumbed to the pressure and India won with six wickets in hand.

This kind of cool and calculated planning made Gavaskar the player and planner he went on to become. A couple of years after that phenomenal victory came another mesmerizing day at The Oval. Target: 421. Gavaskar's partner Chauhan remembers what the Little Master had told him. You can't look at the target as a whole, Chauhan was cautioned. "Sunil kept reminding me not to play any stupid shot and to keep looking for gaps. We almost won the Test."

Gavaskar meant the world to his fans and slow death to the opposition. But what did he mean to the captain under whom he made his Ranji Trophy debut? Ajit Wadekar was the captain when Gavaskar compiled 774 runs in four Tests against the West Indies in their own backyard. That was Gavaskar's debut series.

Says Wadekar, "Frankly speaking, I wasn't expecting great things from Sunny. He was a kid and playing in his first series. It may be recalled that he had missed the first Test of the series due to a finger injury. In those days, whoever scored a century on debut would not score one again. And that's why I didn't want him to. Thankfully, he didn't. I had a lot of confidence in Sunny's abilities and every time he would go to bat, I would say to him, 'Sunny, see you in the evening'. He realized that all the seniors, except Dilip Sardesai, were failing. And that's why he always batted responsibly."

Wadekar remembers how sensitive Gavaskar was. "The seniors used to come late for the team meetings. I told Sunny I would scold him in front of others. The jibe, I assured him, was aimed at the others. Later, he asked me why I treated him unfairly. Eknath Solkar, he reminded me, was as junior to him!"

Vishy had a unique personality: he was sensitive and funny at the same time. "Unlike the others who would get personal while cracking jokes, Vishy had a real sense of humour. I remember in New Delhi in 1969. We won that game. The wicket was dusty and the ball was turning. We were under pressure and our 'reputation' of losing from winning positions was bogging us down. But Vishy played a gem of knock. He was cracking jokes. Perhaps he was enjoying the pressure. His wrist work was superb and every time he played a shot he would smile. He was enjoying the game," Wadekar says.

The cricket necessarily of the highest quality, but the Jubilee Test in February 1980 will go down in history as one of the most iconic India-England contests. The match, organized to commemorate the golden jubilee of the Mumbai Cricket Association, was played at the Wankhede in Mumbai. There are three reasons why this game stands out: Vishwanath's sportsmanship, Ian Botham's mind-blowing show with both bat and ball (6/58, 114 and 7/48) and Bob Taylor's world record of 10 catches.

Skipper Viswanath allowed Taylor to bat on even after umpire Hanumantha Rao adjudged the batsman out caught behind off Kapil Dev at a crucial juncture. Taylor then went to add a game-changing 171 runs for the sixth wicket with Botham. England would go on and win the Test my 10 wickets. Viswanath doesn't regret the incident. "I never regretted it, and I still don't. People are entitled to their opinion but that does not bother me. As a captain, I did what was right at the stage without thinking about the final result. It was clear that Taylor was not out and that was the only thing that mattered," Vishwanath was quoted as saying. "Whatever we would have done in those five days, Botham was just too good and would have probably won it for England," he added.

Vishwanath's 'principles' did annoy his teammates. "We were so cross with him, but quickly realized that it pays to be honest," says Syed Kirmani, the man who took that 'catch'. "Sunny and Dilip (Vengsarkar) were standing next to Vishy in the slip cordon. All of us went up in a flash when Taylor 'nicked' it. The umpire was quick to raise the finger, but Taylor nodded in disappointment. And to everyone's surprise, Vishy walked up to the umpire before asking Taylor to bat on. At the close of play, no one spoke to Vishy about the episode. But three days later, we were very angry. After all, we lost the Test badly," he said.

Karsan Ghavri, who took 5/52 in the first innings of that Test, lavished praise on Vishy and his honesty. "Even if Taylor had edged the ball, Vishy's act will go down in history as one of the best acts of sportsmanship, you see this kind of stuff once in 20-25 years," the left-arm pacer says. "Vishy is a gentleman and he played the game as fair as anyone. Everyone remembers it for being Botham's Test. Yes, it definitely was. But we also got to see the kind of individual Viswanath really was," he said.

Taylor, too, praised Viswanath when he returned to the same ground later. "That was a great gesture of sportsmanship. I can't forget the incident. I thought I would be in trouble. I remember Kapil's confident appeal. The umpire was convinced and I was about to take the long walk back to the pavilion. And suddenly, Vishy came up to me and said he would have a word with the umpire," Taylor recalls.

So how was Gavaskar as captain? He was shrewd, so to speak. He knew what his players were capable of. Just as he loathed losing his wicket, he despised losing a Test match. He played at a time when India had limited resources. He had to rely on Kapil Dev to bowl 25 overs a day innings after innings. When the wicket was not conducive to fast bowling, he would use Kapil sparingly because he was the only match-winning bowler India had.

Did the fear of losing make Gavaskar a defensive captain? No, says Kapil. "I was quite quick when I started my career. But once our world-class spinners retired, Sunny realized that in order to win a Test match, we needed our fast bowlers to operate for longer periods. And had I continued to bowl fast, Sunny's plans wouldn't have materialized. He convinced me that I wouldn't last long. He told me not to bowl so quick match after match."

Gavaskar believed in brains, not brawn. He focused on strategizing and reading the psyche of the opposition. He made Kapil pay attention to the psychology of a batsman facing a fast bowler. Such smart tactics made him a good player. Says Kapil, "How to get a batsman out was something Gavaskar taught me."

Sunny and Vishy seem like the two ends of a spectrum. One was calculative and stern, the other carefree and joyful. Of course, any attempt to compare the two is way too tempting. After all, both are legends. But really, it would be stupid to say one was better than the other. Says Wadekar, "I really don't know the reason why Vishy, with all the strokes that he had, wasn't as consistent as Sunny. But for the sheer joy of watching the art of batting, Vishy was way ahead of the others."

Wadekar's quote is enough to put all comparisons and contrasts at rest. They had different roles to play: one held up an end, fortifying the team; the other was allowed to express himself.

If Viswanath was sober (as a person, that is), Gavaskar, at times, exhibited volatile behavior. He had the guts to take the establishment on. And because he was a consistent performer, neither the selectors nor the BCCI could take him to task. In the inaugural World Cup, in 1975, Gavaskar scored an unbeaten 36 in a 60-over game! Even his teammates couldn't fathom what was going on. He never made any attempt to step up the scoring rate. The manager of the Indian team, former captain GS Ramchand, censored him in his report, but the BCCI didn't act.

In 1981, at the Melbourne Cricket Ground, he staged a walkout after he was apparently given out leg-before. He was seen pointing to the umpire that he had played the ball. And as he was reluctantly walking towards the dressing room, he was provoked by the Aussies. He then dragged his opening partner towards the pavilion. What was his intention? We would never know because if both had crossed the boundary line, the umpires would have been well within their rights to award the match to Australia. Sensing the gravity of the situation, team manager Wing Commander Durrani sent Chauhan back and a major international controversy was avoided.

Sunny and Vishy were different but their goals were the same. What does an aspiring cricketer learn from this? Nail yourself to an end and not look at the scoreboard like Sunny? Or be like Vishy and bat like your life depends on it? The very fact that both approaches yielded success teaches us only one thing: it doesn't matter what style you have, if it's yours and you if believe in it, you will do well. The Sunny-Vishy affair of Indian Test cricket is a story of belief. Those who watched them were fortunate.

Dilip Vengsarkar

Mohinder Amarnath

'LORD OF LORD'S'

Practice makes a cricketer perfect. That's what they all have been saying for years. And that's what the players have been religiously doing – practising day in and day out. Practice is all about perseverance. Diligent practice hones your technique. That said, how do you develop guts? Is there a training regimen that makes you gutsy?

Obviously not.

So how does a batsman act like a wall when his team is in trouble?

No Guts, No Glory

A few psychologists have tried their hand at helping people 'develop' guts. They came up with mental conditioning drills that would help a cricketer exhibit guts on the field of play. What do the legends of the game have to say about this 'injection' of guts? "Utter bullshit", says Sir Viv Richards.

The West Indian faced the fastest of bowlers without a helmet. Green tops, bouncy pitches, rank turners, dead strips... nothing mattered when Richards was at the crease. None of this affected his confidence levels. Try and scare him with a bouncer and he'd hook or pull you. That's guts. This is one trait you can't 'develop'. You either have it or you don't. Mohinder 'Jimmy' Amarnath and Dilip Vengsarkar did not take any classes to become gutsy. They were born tough. All they cared for was about playing.

Amarnath had grown up idolizing his father, Lala Amarnath. And the boy grew up to become like his father – formidable, courageous, inventive and, of course, outspoken. Vengsarkar was brought up on a heavy dose of street-smart cricket in the gullies of Dadar. His backyard, the Hindu Colony, was a haven for cricket.

Amarnath was like a puzzle, like the one in your newspaper. He was different every day, almost incomprehensible. His form was as unpredictable as the English weather: one day he'd display enviable guts and maturity beyond his years, the very next match, he'd resemble a gawky schoolboy all at sea. This unfortunate level of inconsistency, perhaps, explains why Amarnath played just 69 Test matches in a career that spanned 20 years. He made his debut as early as the year 1969. He was just 18 when he took guard against the Aussies. But after that series, he disappeared from the scene only to return six years later for the 1975-76 tour of New Zealand.

Actually, it was not entirely Amarnath's fault that he didn't play for six years. The team was loaded with seniors then. The team that created history on the twin tours of the West Indies and England in 1970-71 had some big names. The player Amarnath had to outshine to stake a claim for a Test berth was all-rounder S Abid Ali. But the experienced man left no scope for competition.

The coin fell in Amarnath's favour when the selectors were contemplating the inclusion of an all-rounder instead of a second wicketkeeper (Syed Kirmani) for the 1971 tour of England. They had to wait as Farokh Engineer, the first-choice glovesman, was awaiting clearance from his bosses at Lancashire to release him for the series in England. They let Engineer go, but it was Kirmani who was picked for the side games.

Again, in the 1972-73 series, Amarnath managed to get a foot in the door when requirement was a medium pacer. But Abid Ali and Eknath Solkar filled in whenever the spinners weren't in operation. Still no luck. He would soon realize that patience is a virtue.

He finally got a look-in, in 1975. He was picked for the New Zealand and West Indies series. 'The Comeback Man', as he rightly was called, Amarnath played from 1975 to 1988. The highlight of his career was the series in Pakistan when Imran Khan bamboozled the entire line-up. Amarnath clearly stood out, scoring three brilliant centuries. He went on to score three more against the West Indies.

Apart from these two sojourns, where he made jaws drop, Amarnath never looked like the batsman who'd tackled Imran and Malcolm Marshall. In fact, when the West Indies arrived in India, Amarnath's sequence of scores resembled the pin code of some obscure town. He made 0, 0, 1, 0, 0, 0 in 6 innings of 3 Tests.

In the West Indies, the bowlers tried to bounce him out and he relished the challenge. The more they bounced him, the more he would play the hook shot. In those days, there was no limit on the number of bouncers. And the West Indians would happily bowl at the batsman's head. They would keep a man at deep fine-leg and another one at deep square-leg. They encouraged Amarnath to hook. And our man would take them on. When the same lot of bowlers arrived in India for a series, they altered the strategy. Seeing Amarnath's two-eyed stance, they kept pitching it up and getting the ball to come in. As they kept succeeding in getting his wicket first ball, Amarnath began to lose confidence. Cricket is a great leveler, they say. After six failures, Amarnath had to be dropped.

Lala couldn't see his son play any other sport than cricket. Says Amarnath, "He would plan everything, from the practice schedule to matches. He was knowledgeable and that helped me a lot. To him, hard work mattered. Even in winters, my brothers and I had to be present at the ground early in the morning. I never saw my father play, but I've heard a lot of stories about him, and those stories really inspired me."

Kapil Dev played a lot with Amarnath. "Jimmy was a gutsy batsman. Had he been as technically perfect as some reputed batsman, he would have been a big asset to the team. He had the guts but, in international cricket, you need to have a sound technique to survive. I witnessed his six centuries – three each in Pakistan and the West Indies. Bowl short to him and he'd go after it. Fortunately for us, he was in great form throughout the 1983 World Cup," Dev says.

Aunshuman Gaekwad was another of Amarnath's long-time friend. They'd played together in the Vizzy Trophy (inter-university zonal tournament). "He wasn't a flamboyant cricketer, but a sensible one. A very good student of the game, Jimmy was a very useful all-rounder that any team would like to have. As a batsman, he was gutsy and stubborn, calm and very, very hardworking. I will never forget his knock in Barbados," Gaekwad says.

Gaekwad adds, "During that knock in Barbados, he was hit on the face and required stitches. Jimmy came back and hooked Marshall for a four off the first delivery. This was his approach, but he liked to play long innings. It was unfortunate that Jimmy had so many breaks in his international career. Hats off to him, though, for fighting his way back into the side. I was very certain that his fitness levels would always hold him in good stead. He was outspoken and so was his batting."

Amarnath's biggest strength was that he was ready to work hard. Born with a silver spoon and to a cricketing father who would eventually be known as the 'Grand Old Man of Indian Cricket', he was never prepared to 'inherit' his place in the Indian team. He earned it. And thanks to Lala's outspoken nature (during his playing days and later as selector and manager), the establishment took it out on Jimmy. But the son never gave up. He kept making comebacks.

Vengsarkar, too, had his ups and downs. His progress chart at Dadar Union can, at best, be called unstable. But Vengsarkar realized very soon that he had to make a mark. He understood he had to change his approach to batting. An attacking batsman who featured in the middle order for Mumbai in the Ranji Trophy, he was so impressive that he was picked for the unofficial Test against Sri Lanka as an opener.

As a schoolboy, he kept wickets and continued to do so for his college and university. There was no special reason for a tall player like him to stand behind the stumps. Neither his school nor his college coach bothered to think of the repercussions the job would have on his frail physique. The worst part was that he gave the impression he wasn't enjoying it.

On his local performance he was drafted in the Mumbai team to play against Gujarat. He was crestfallen and seen sobbing as he was out for zero. Mumbai cricket is tough. Teary eyes don't get sympathy. Perform or perish is the simple mantra. But in Vengsarkar's case, the talent was immense and everybody was hoping that he will come good.

With his upright stance, Vengsarkar had the ability to pick the length of the ball early. By thrusting his front foot forward, he would caress the ball through the off-side. His on-drive was very delectable. Being tall, he had a very good reach and that enabled him to smother the spin or drive on the up.

In 1974, fast bowler Pandurang Salgaonkar was a rage in domestic circles. Several leading Indian batsmen found him too hot to handle. In the Duleep Trophy matches against South Zone, he captured five wickets in each innings on a turning track, unmindful of the fact that the batsmen he was bowling to were India's very best: MAK Pataudi and GR Viswanath among others.

Soon as a lanky teenager walked to the middle, the crowd wondered how soon he would perish. The lad had opened with Subhash Bandiwadekar against New Hind club at the PJ Hindu Gymkhana. Salgaonkar, meanwhile, looked threatening from the first ball he bowled to this teenager. The wicket keeper of National club was standing on the practice plot close to the boundary on the northern side.

But this 18-year-old batsman was different. His gait showed he was least concerned about the attacking field that was set for him. Repeatedly going on the front foot, he played on the up displaying some majestic drives on either sides. Every time he drove, the next ball was pitched short and it would find the square-leg boundary. The faster the ball came, the quicker it disappeared. With those 86 runs, Dilip Vengsarkar had announced his arrival with a thunder.

Watching Vengsarkar bat was always a delight. But there is one knock the pundits can never stop praising. It was an Irani Cup tie against the likes of Bedi and Prasanna, at Nagpur.

Operation Demolition

In retrospect, it was amusing that he was inducted into the Mumbai team at the last minute. Mumbai lost three early wickets in their pursuit of Rest of India's 210. Vengsarkar, then a teenager, joined the seasoned Ashok Mankad in the middle. His boyish charm worked well against two champion bowlers who were known for their flight. They employed every possible trick to lure him out of the crease.

Vengsarkar did as he was taught. When the ball is flighted, step out and hit it over the top. It was his day. Every time, Bedi and Prasanna dragged him out of the cease, Vengsarkar danced down the wicket and sent the ball soaring over the boundary. Smashing 7 towering sixes

and 11 fours, Vengsarkar entertained the crowd to no end. Lala Amarnath was so pleased that he gave him the nickname 'Colonel' because the young man reminded him of Colonel CK Nayudu, India's first captain, who played for the Holkars but was born in the Orange City.

Though the knock was special, he got into a habit of hitting in the air. His three digit knocks were less. The selectors were looking for such consistent knocks. Soon, Vengarskar was considered the best batsman of fast bowling. There was something in him that the other Indian batsmen lacked. Says Vengsarkar, "It was practice against quality fast bowlers at Dadar Union that helped me succeed. It taught me to play pacers square off the wicket. Very early in my career, I faced one of the quickest fast bowlers, Michael Holding, in the Jamaica Test. There was a ridge on the pitch and many Indian players got hit. But I played fearlessly, but on the merit of the ball. I didn't think about the ridge."

After that tour, Vengsarkar was a different batsman. As Kapil Dev says, "Vengsarkar was a thorough professional and, like a typical Mumbai player, he would put a huge price on his wicket."

To put a big price on one's wicket is something even Amarnath did. But while batting, he would give hope to the bowler who would, in turn, bounce him. When he was in form in 1982, he scored 1,182 runs in 11 Tests. But in the following season, he scored one run in six innings!

A 'Heady' Cocktail

But Amarnath had become the darling of the masses after his knocks in the 1977 Melbourne Test. He was batting confidently when he tried to hook Sam Gannon. The ball hit his temple. He was carried off the field. The impact was severe, but Amarnath didn't panic. He just let the doctors do their job. Any other player would have had second thoughts about batting again. But this man was in a hurry to forget his pain. He wanted to send across a message. He went out to bat after lunch. And by the time he was dismissed, Amarnath had made 90.

He wasn't done. In order to make up for those 10 runs, Amarnath scored a century in the second innings. But the cricketing fraternity was eventually proved right. A compulsive hooker, Amarnath became an easy target. He got out to terrible shots. Bowlers knew how to get him. They'd place a fielder at deep fine-leg and Amarnath would often oblige. When he timed it well, it would go for six. But on slow Indian wickets, he was easy meat.

After the Australian tour, Amarnath went to Pakistan. India were playing their neighbours after a gap of 17 years. Amarnath was at the receiving end of an array of bouncers, this time from Imran Khan. One ball hit him on the back of the head. Amarnath was newly married. His wife, a psychiatrist, was obviously worried. In fact, everybody but Amaranth was tense. He did the same thing, walking into bat with gusto. The bouncers kept coming. And while trying to hook one such bouncer, Amarnath tripped and fell on the stumps.

A dismissal of that sort was enough for people to start questioning his abilities. In 1976 at the Wankhede, against the New Zealand, he walked in sporting his father's sola hat, last used in the 1940s. But the hat did little to sort out his problem with short-pitched stuff. He was hit on the hat.

A man who was never scared to get back on the field even after a head injury, was now deflated. He loved hooking the fastest bowlers, but it wasn't the same any more. Amarnath started doubting himself. He was on the verge of losing his place in the team. And when India toured Australia in 1980-81, he wasn't on the plane.

But Amarnath wasn't called a fighter for nothing. He continued to score heavily in domestic cricket. Despite his consistent performances, two other Mumbai players were accommodated in the national team. Even that didn't deter him. He bagged a ticket for the tour of Pakistan and, there he was, back again in business.

In cricket, your biggest strength is also your biggest weakness. Most batsmen, you'd see, get out playing their favourite shot. When a batsman employs, say, the cut on a regular basis, the opposition prepares accordingly. The point region is protected like an international border and the bowlers bowl to a plan. When 11 brains work against one, you know who'd win. Amarnath's obsession with the hook was something similar.

Comebacks are more difficult than they seem. Not only has a player got to compete with his own self, but also with the other competitors. Every year, a fresh bunch of young performers compete. And because they have age on their side, the selectors tend to lean towards them. When Amarnath was scoring runs in Ranji Trophy, a young stylish middle-order batsman from Hyderabad burst on to the scene.

Armed with an unorthodox style, Mohammad Azharuddin was toying with bowlers. And he was also an electrifying fielder. Soon, there were whispers that India had found Amarnath's replacement. However, in the Irani Cup tie prior to the Pakistan series, Azharuddin fell for a duck to Balvinder Singh Sandhu. Amarnath responded with a big score, got selected and the rest, as they say, is history.

Self-belief: A Huge Weapon

Here's Sandhu's testimony to Amarnath's methods. "On the 1982-83 tour of Pakistan, I wasn't picked for the first three Tests. I would bowl a lot in the nets. Jimmy would treat the net sessions like a match. And because Imran was bowling sharp in-swingers, Jimmy would tell me to bowl the same. So focused was Jimmy at the nets that beating him was impossible. He scored three hundred on that tour. Everybody else, except Gavaskar, failed on that tour."

If Amarnath was gutsy, so was Vengsarkar. His bravado, however, was of a different kind. Facing the likes of Holding, Marshall, Thomson and Imran required guts. Vengsarkar had loads of it. What he also possessed was the ability to score a bucketful of runs, series after series. The conditions in England would send a chill down anyone's spine, but Vengsarkar relished the challenge. He became the first overseas cricketer to score three consecutive hundreds at Lord's.

The secret behind Vengsarkar's consistency was his self-belief. This is something Amarnath lacked. Amarnath's confidence was fickle. When in form, he would bat with supreme confidence. But once the runs dried up, he'd be a deflated man.

Vengsarkar was a typical Mumbai cricketer who knew how much the team relied on him, Gavaskar and Viswanath. Hooking was risky and he refused to play that shot. However, he didn't fail to go for it when the opportunity presented itself. In the West Indies, Marshall attacked Vengsarkar from around the wicket, only to be hooked mercilessly.

Vengsarkar always played according to the situation. He would seamlessly fit into any role. When India played at home, they would prepare turning wickets. One had to be technically sound to bat on those treacherous pitches. Just as Peter May and Colin Cowdrey negated the turn of mystery bowler Sony Ramadhin by thrusting their front pads during the 1958 series, Vengsarkar mastered the art of pad-play to frustrate the spinners.

During the 1978 Mumbai Test against Pakistan, India were in trouble having lost half the side for less than 50. Anything not in line with the stumps was padded away. But if a ball was to be driven, Vengsarkar did so with élan. Basically an on-side player, he developed his backfoot play on his first tour of England where hitting off the front foot wasn't possible all the time. As he said, he began to play square off the wicket to minimize the risk.

Connoisseurs believe Vengsarkar shouldn't have changed his game. They say had he not altered his approach, he would have scored a few thousand runs more. However, cricket isn't a game of ifs and buts. A single delivery can determine a batsman's career. Vengsarkar would be the first to admit that he ought to have amassed more runs than he did.

Vengsarkar wasn't the only one to blame for this. The selectors were also at fault. Seldom were they fair to him. During the Bangalore Test against Pakistan in the 1983-84 series, the selection committee asked Vengsarkar to open the innings. He politely declined, only to be inconsiderately dropped. Did he regret his decision? Did it matter to him? Not one bit. He continued to perform.

At Sharjah, prior to the tour of England, team manager Raj Singh Dungarpur made it clear that Vengsarkar didn't fit in his scheme of things. Our man took the snub in his stride. But in England, he had to be picked. And he responded by scoring another hundred at Lord's.

Braving the treatment that was meted to him, Vengsarkar kept delivering. Ask him about his favourite knock and he goes into deep thought. "I played many in a career of 116 Tests. The knocks I played in low-scoring games were more satisfying. Definitely, the one at Headingley in 1986 was a good one. Not because I hit a century, but because it helped India win the Test. The ball was moving and I had to be cautious."

Chetan Chauhan was much senior to Vengsarkar, but they were thick as thieves. Says Chauhan, "Like Sunil (Gavaskar), Dilip curtailed his shots because we had a long tail. We had only five international batsmen. Our spinners batted very badly. If we had a team like we have nowadays, Dilip would have been able to play his shots much more freely because he was a natural striker of the ball. Later, after I went out of the team in 1981, he did play some good innings. But if he was backed by the team management and given confidence, he would have got more hundreds. He had the technique and, more importantly, he had the temperament."

Vengsarkar was what you'd call a born fighter. Knock him down and he'd crawl his way up, much like Rocky Balboa, and unleash himself on the opponent. For the better part of his career, Vengsarkar was India's 'Crisis Specialist'. He was also the world's top-ranked batsman when computerized rankings were introduced.

Vengsarkar was a man for all seasons. After a great playing career, he served the country as chairman of the senior national selection committee. Vengsarkar knew how important it was to the earlier blood players. The likes of MS Dhoni, Virat Kohli and others have proved his theory right.

We know of several retired players who don't really care about giving anything back to the game. Most of them are busy adding zeroes to their bank balance. Vengsarkar is an exception.

He started a foundation and launched an academy at the Oval Maidan. Later, he opened cricket schools in Chembur and Pune. He does not charge a penny, mind you. In fact, he pays for the players' education and travel apart from providing them with free kits. Vengsarkar has a great eye for talent. He does not go merely by the numbers. His 'roving' eyes can spot talent.

As the chairman of the Talent, Research and Development Wing (TRDW) of the BCCI, he went around the country hunting for talent with the help of his wing officers. The project yielded talented young cricketers from all over country. Dhoni happens to be one of them.

One Comeback Too Many

Amarnath was tired of making comebacks. There was no respite, no relief. He was never a permanent member of the side. The man who was known for his ability to bounce back had finally lost patience. The dodo doll was tired of being dropped and getting up.

The final chapter was the selection committee meeting prior to the 1987-88 series against the West Indies. He was asked to be present in Chandigarh as captain. BCCI secretary Ranbir Singh Mahendra said he hadn't invited him. Apparently, the board had invited Vengsarkar.

This episode was highly insulting. It was no ordinary thing for Amarnath. He was leading the team his father once led. Eventually, he was dropped for the New Zealand series. All that came out of Amarnath's tired lips was, "the selectors are a bunch of jokers". With that statement, his international career came to an end. No more waiting, no more trying.

It is sad that a sportsman of his caliber ended up being a puppet in the hands of the so-called custodians of the game.

But Amarnath and Vengsarkar continued to have faith in themselves. While Vengsarkar never lost confidence, Amarnath did. But even then, he never lost faith. He knew he could make a comeback. And he did it, time and again.

These gentlemen represent hope.

Kapil Dev

Ravi Shastri

That day, the Brabourne Stadium was bathed in sunshine. The boys, all in whites, were too excited to notice the fact that they were sweating profusely. It was the summer of 1974 and Hemu Adhikari was the man in charge of the BCCI camp.

The boys weren't in Mumbai for trials. They had already proved their worth. They were here to show that they could put it to some use. The lanky lads were getting ready for practice.

It was time for the customary 'please introduce yourself' session. One by one, the teenagers did as they were told. "Roger Binny", "Shivlal Yadav", "Yograj Singh", "Milind Gunjal", "Raju Jadeja". And then it was the turn of "Kapil Dev Nikhanj". The others giggled. Why? Did it have to do with his high-pitched voice?

He was all confidence and his voice signalled his intent. The camp was not a Mumbai darshan for him. The next six weeks were to decide his fate. He had just arrived from Chandigarh, the great city planned by the likes of Le Corbusier, Pierre Jeanneret, Jane Drew and Maxwell Fry.

Chandigarh is a lovely city. But those days it had just one respectable cricket ground – the Sector 16 Stadium. For Kapil, training at the Brabourne stadium was like a dream come true. And as he and the others paid attention to Adhikari, they got a fair idea of how the next six weeks would pan out. "No water during practice," the coach announced. "Nothing at all." This wasn't going to be fun. Kapil realized that soon enough.

The announcement was met with grumbles and murmurs. Kapil and the other lad from Chandigarh,

Yograj Singh Bundhel, were particularly appalled at the "no water" diktat. The food wasn't great either: just two chappatis and dal after a hard day's work.

Kapil's diet was obviously more wholesome. After a strenuous practice session in the morning, he confronted Keki Tarapore, who was then secretary of the Cricket Club of India. The former Bombay player questioned Kapil in the presence of the others. "Kapil, I am told you don't like the food we give you." Kapil replied, "I don't like it, Sir. I am a fast bowler and I need more food. I need good food and more solid food."

For a moment, Kapil was hopeful. He thought Tarapore would get the point. But our man laughed out loud. "There are no fast bowlers in India," he sneered at Kapil. The boy was hurt. And on that day, he promised himself he'd become the best Indian fast bowler of all time.

Tarapore must be credited for provoking Kapil. Those words gave India what years of yearning couldn't: a genuine pace bowler. Even then, we watched a revised version of Kapil bowling day in day out in the heat and humidity of Mumbai. And mind you, he didn't have any water at all. One could see that he was ready to give it all. He looked every inch a genuine all-rounder. And the healthy competition between him and Yograj only made him better.

Kapil never looked back since that fateful day. His strides were long and rapid. He always had the talent, but knew how important it was to work hard. There was no method in his madness. His coach, Desh Prem Azad, would make his trainees sweat it out at the Sector 16 Stadium. Fitness was paramount.

While Kapil was training hard to reach the heights no Indian cricketer had, Ravi Shastri's fate was sealed. He was destined to play for India since the day he was born. It's just that it happened a little earlier than we expected. Studying in Mumbai's Don Bosco High School, Shastri got the opportunity to represent the Matunga outfit in the penultimate year at school. His school lost in the final of the prestigious Giles Shield tournament, but the lanky chap impressed many. The following year, Don Bosco won the championship.

This is how Shastri started his journey. Ambitious as he was, Shastri realized that in the cricket-crazy city of Mumbai he needed more than just talent to survive. In those days, there weren't any age-group tournaments for teenagers. Barely 17, Shastri walked into a selection trial for Under-22 players. A large number of youth were present with their birth certificates. They had to prove they weren't a day older than 22. Shastri, though, had things to worry about.

The selectors stood watched as batsman after batsman faced 10 deliveries each. Shastri batted confidently, smashing the bowlers all over the place. When he was asked to bowl left-arm spin on that dampish pitch, his deliveries turned and bounced.

As he stood there listening to an official announce the list of probables, he realized that he hadn't made the cut. "I felt gutted," he says. But he didn't give up. Turning out for the Karnataka Sporting Association in local tournaments, he played a major role as an all-rounder against champion teams. One fine day, he received a call to attend the nets of

Nirlon, a corporate team led by Sunil Gavaskar. Gavaskar liked what he saw and asked the Mumbai selectors to include Shastri in the team for the knockout match against Bihar.

No one but Gavaskar had seen Shastri ply his trade. Shastri's life changed for good when he got a call from BCCI in the middle of a Ranji match in Lucknow. India's main spinner, Dilip Doshi, was injured and it was time for the tour of New Zealand.

It wasn't that Shastri hadn't performed in the Ranji Trophy. In his debut season, he had picked up six wickets for 61 runs in the final against Delhi. He was already on the radar of the Indian team management. But the fact that Gavaskar, the India captain, took a liking to his potential certainly helped.

He wasn't known for his batting prowess earlier. He would bat at No. 10. "When I went for the Mumbai Under-22 trials, I got to face only 10 balls and I smashed them all. And while bowling, I made batsmen much bigger in age and size dance to my tunes. At 17, I realized that it would be very difficult to get to bat at the top. So I grabbed every chance I got to bat as night watchman. I used to bat at No. 10 even for Mumbai University. One fine day, vice-captain Ghulam Parkar urged the captain to promote me to No. 3," Shastri says.

There's a turning point, a spark, in the life of every sportsperson. The one in Shastri's career came about when he was playing in Lucknow. "We were playing against Uttar Pradesh and I had bagged a pair. I was crestfallen. Skipper Ashok Mankad looked me in the eye and said, 'Ravi, remember the light at the end of the tunnel will be at its brightest'. And that very day, I received a call asking me to join the Indian team in New Zealand as Dilip Doshi was injured."

Though he was to replace Doshi, he was very keen to bat higher up the order. He knew that he wouldn't be getting to bat in the nets. "I looked to bat as a night watchman. That way, I could impress the captain and others."

From 1932 till 2013, no Indian opener has scored two Test centuries in a series in England. Renowned openers like Vijay Merchant, Mushtaq Ali, Vinoo Mankad, Sunil Gavaskar, Virender Sehwag and Gautam Gambhir haven't managed this.

Shastri was always considered a stop-gap arrangement when it came to opening the innings, yet he averaged around 45 at the top. That's second only to Gavaskar's 51.12. Specialized openers like Chetan Chauhan (31.58), Aunshuman Gaekwad (30.08) and Krishnamachari Srikkanth (29.88) stand far behind. Shastri is also the first Indian cricketer to score a double century in a Test match Down Under. And he is the first Asian to score two centuries in a series and one double hundred as an opener.

For a player who was not known to be attacking, he scored an unbeaten 200 in 113 minutes and 123 balls against Baroda. His knock was studded with 13 sixes and as many fours. It was the fastest double hundred in first class cricket.

What was easily noticeable and yet remarkable was that Shastri knew his limitations and played within himself. His special 'chappati' shot on the leg side fetched him a lot of runs. He seemed to believe in the maxim that if one stayed at the wicket long enough, the runs would certainly come. But to stay at the wicket, you need perseverance and courage.

Shastri was soon asked to open. But the men bowling to him were Sarfraz Nawaz and Imran Khan. These bowlers weren't just skillful; they were deadly. And with some help from local umpires Kizar Hayat and Shakoor Rana, they did everything in their power to ensure the ball reversed. But Shastri was efficient in his own way. He was a tenacious batsman. "Opening the innings for me was a challenge and I was positive at the crease. Yes, the fast bowlers were very good and umpiring in Pakistan was always dicey. But I got a hundred," he remembers.

Balvinder Singh Sandhu and Shastri go back a long way. The medium pacer remembers the circumstances in which Gavaskar had asked Shastri to open. It wasn't a fairytale setting. "Shastri had injured the webbing of his bowling arm. He hadn't played much and when he did, he didn't perform. I was sitting with him when Gavaskar came up and said, 'Ravi, will you open?'"

Shastri was in a dilemma. He always wanted to take his batting seriously. Here was his chance. But he was injured. "I knew him since our university days. We were pretty close. And I convinced him to open. Mentally, Ravi was very, very tough," says Sandhu.

On the 1982-83 tour of Pakistan, Shastri had to compete with Dilip Doshi and Maninder Singh, both left-arm spinners. He was dropped from the XI after a dismal showing in the First Test at Lahore.

After that, he hardly got a look-in. He looked set to warm the bench in the final Test at Karachi too. The Caribbean tour was up next, but Shastri's chances of making the team seemed remote. And yet, a couple of days before the final Test, Gavaskar posed that tricky question. "Ravi was in a quandary; he could hardly grip the bat with his injured hand and had to bat and bowl extraordinarily well to find a place in the team for the Caribbean tour. That evening, we discussed the issue threadbare and both of us agreed that the opportunity to open was Godsend," Sandhu says.

In Karachi, Shastri lost his skipper and opening partner early. However, he batted on for hours, scoring 128 runs. Those were precious runs because Shastri had to deal with the reverse-swing of the Pakistani pace-bowling machine which had mastered the art of doctoring the ball. Their bowlers and fielders would help get the ball into "proper shape" by picking the seam and scratching the surface with fingernails or bottle crowns. "Shastri's grit kept him going and his knock in Karachi was full of guts and gumption. It changed the course of his career. He later bowled 22 overs for a solitary wicket in the drawn Test."

While India had just found a tenacious all-rounder, Kapil continued to be a carefree batsman. At times, he played breathtaking shots. It made people wonder why he wasn't taking his batting a little more seriously. Skipper Gavaskar tried putting some sense into Kapil's head by telling him that he batted discreetly, he could get some important runs for the team. But Kapil was of the opinion that altering his natural game would deprive him of the few runs he was scoring. And after his century against the West Indies in New Delhi, he and many others, were convinced that his approach was just fine. Gavaskar's suggestion was thus ignored.

Kapil's batting style worried Gavaskar. He wrote in a magazine that Kapil would not score a half century in Test cricket. "I had spoken to him in the dressing room, at dinners and at every other opportunity, but he would continue to play cameos that were enthralling, but which were all too brief not only for the crowd but also for the team," Gavaskar wrote.

People had seen Kapil's determination, flamboyance and confidence. That day, they saw his anger. A day prior to the Mumbai Test against Pakistan in 1979, one saw an angry Kapil. Gavaskar had written that "at the moment, Kapil can't be considered an all-rounder because he bats like a lower-order batsman". The very next day, India was playing on a rank turner and the Pakistani spinners were making merry. Batting at No. 8, Kapil scored a brilliant 69. Kapil attacked the spinners with his glorious drives.

How about that epic 175-run knock against Zimbabwe in the 1983 World Cup? India were reduced to 4 down 9 and then 5 down 17. Unfortunate, that match wasn't telecast live, but those who watched it from close quarters call it the best display of batting ever. Syed Kirmani was at the non-striker's end for the better part of Kapil's unbeaten innings. "What do you want me to describe when someone scores 175 after his team was 5 down for 17?" Kirmani retorts.

Sandhu has something more to offer. "I was witness to two of Kapil's performances which changed the history of Indian cricket, nay sport itself," he says. The first knock is, of course, the one against Zimbabwe at Tunbridge Wells. Sandhu remembers how Kapil carried India into semifinals. Dev walked in and stemmed the rot with some help from

Roger Binny and Madan Lal.

Once he got his eye in, Kapil started annihilating the Zimbabwe bowlers, one by one. He mercilessly clobbered six sixes and sixteen fours.

"His unbeaten 175 shell-shocked the Zimbabweans and India sailed into the semifinals somewhat comfortably. During that historic knock, I was sitting in the dressing room with a hot cup of coffee to keep myself warm and hoping that India would at least reach a fighting score. When lunch was announced, India was still not out of the woods. And Kapil walked into the dressing room only to be welcomed by deathly silence. The atmosphere was almost like a funeral. 'C'mon guys!' he said. 'We've got to fight it out. The match isn't over yet. All of you better have your lunch. We can't fight back on empty stomachs'!

These words lifted the boys and the team felt like wanting to do well for their captain who was leading from the front.

"That knock of his will be remembered as one of the finest of all time. It is indeed sad that this epic innings was not recorded for posterity as BBC TV was on strike that day. Gavaskar was so impressed that he greeted him halfway to the pavilion with a glass of water. Mr SK Wankhede, the BCCI president, was there too. He ordered his chauffeur not to leave the ground when he saw us reduced to 5 down 17. As things turned out, he had to wait till late evening to see the last Zimbabwean wicket tumble," recounts Sandhu.

Kapil arrived on the international cricket as a fast bowler who was actually – and surprisingly fast by Indian standards. He was always fascinated by speed. The nature

of the pitch didn't bother him. He had a smooth run-up and a lovely sideways action. His coach never tried to tinker with his action. "Remain fit, bowl more and bowl fast." That is all he aspired to do. And that is what he did, time and again. Bowl more, bowl fast. He would practise with purpose. He had a natural out-swinger that squared up many a batsman.

Gavaskar realized that if he had to use Kapil as a strike bowler, he needed to conserve his energy. His workload (about 20 overs per innings) and the pace at which he bowled could have made him a spent force within in a couple of years. Gavaskar had tried his best to convince Kapil about his batting. But he didn't give up. He was ready to make Kapil understand the importance of saving his best as a bowler.

Thankfully for Gavaskar, Kapil was easier to convince this time around. He realized that batsmen have the tendency to play out the fast bowlers in international cricket. And with quite a few matches being played on placid pitches, he needed to be accurate. To get his length right all the time, he had to have control over the movement of the ball. With this change in approach, he became more effective.

"Kapil is India's greatest match-winner and he could do it with both bat and ball. And as we saw in the final of the 1983 World Cup, he could turn the game around with his fielding ability as well. He was awesome with the bat, but he did not fully utilize his talent. Instead, he chose to concentrate on spearheading a limited bowling attack," Gavaskar says.

Ironically they had agreed to disagree during their playing days. India beat David Gower's England side in the first Test match at the Wankhede in 1984-85 series. On the fifth day of the second Test in New Delhi, the match seemed to be heading for a draw. The hosts had wiped out England's 111-run first-innings lead and were cruising at 207/4 with a little over a session to go. That's when Sandeep Patil holed out in the deep. In walked Kapil Dev who being a senior member of the team was expected to bat responsibly.

For some strange reason, Kapil Dev played an irresponsible shot. He tried to hit every ball out of the park. It was frustrating not only to the team members and the selectors but even the crowd was wondering what he was up to. He managed to hit a six and collect a single before getting out to Pat Pocock. One thing led to another and India lost their last six wickets for just 28 runs. England knocked off the required runs with ease.

Gavaskar was obviously angry at Patil and Kapil. It was understandable. After all, they had no business to bat they way they did. A Test match was lost. Just like that. And when the selection committee, headed by Chandu Borde, consulted the captain before picking the side for the following Test match, the expected happened. Both Patil and Kapil were promptly dropped.

What followed was murky. While Kapil blamed Gavaskar for his ouster, the skipper held his ground saying he was late for the meeting and played no role whatsoever in the entire saga. It was then left to BCCI president NKP Salve to summon the legends and persuade them to shake hands again.

Gavaskar and Kapil continued to love and hate each other. And they exchanged the captaincy once again. And the former's decision to drop down the order during India's tour of Sri Lanka did not amuse Kapil. The two great men later said on record that the press blew the whole thing out of proportion. Truth is they still remain good friends. In fact Gavaskar maintains that Kapil is India's greatest and most talented cricketer ever.

Interestingly, the BCCI roped in Gavaskar to be part of the Indian Premier League council after media mogul Subhash Chandra named Kapil the brand ambassador of the now-defunct Indian Cricket League.

Meanwhile, Shastri was turning into a gem of a player. Being tall, his high-arm action helped him extract bounce. Shastri varied his pace and line. He didn't have to flight the ball as he stood well over six feet. Shastri impressed further because of his ability to adapt.

Yes, Kapil won India the 1983 World Cup, but he wasn't exactly a successful captain. And he's the first to admit this. He became captain after Gavaskar was unceremoniously sacked after India lost to Pakistan in 1983. The team looked shaky and inexperienced and Kapil looked the only certainty. He knew he was too inexperienced to lead the side. He was an instinctive all-rounder who enjoyed his game. Looking after 10 other players was not his cup of tea. He was in the Garfield Sobers mould. He believed that as an all-rounder, he must be able to take more responsibility.

But Shastri's all-round credentials were much more solid as he was a shrewd thinker of the game. He was a keen observer of tactics and he learnt a lot from Ashok Mankad and Gavaskar. In the only Test that he captained against the West Indies in Chennai, he displayed his tactical acumen. Leg-spinner Narendra Hirwani, who took 16 wickets on debut, compared Shastri with MS Dhoni. "Ravi was my first Test captain. Frankly speaking, I was nervous. For leg spinners to succeed in any format of cricket, they require the confidence of the captain. I had known him, but Test cricket was a different ball-game. He advised me not to use all my variations in the first innings because he wanted me to be the main bowler on the fifth day. Viv Richards was batting confidently and was not out overnight with 50-odd to his name. I told Ravi that had I bowled the flipper, I would have got Richards and a few others out. The next morning, Ravi gave me the ball first up and I had Richards bowled."

Shastri was surely a bowler's captain. Says Hirwani, "At Sharjah in 1988, he told me 'Hiru, bowl like a king. I don't care how many runs you give away in 10 overs. I want two to three wickets from you. I picked up 11 wickets in three games. He would give us bowlers a lot of confidence because he knew we could win him matches."

Shastri scored 11 Test hundreds but even then he was never considered a genuine opener. Incredibly, he scored a 100 and a 187 during India's tour of England in 1990. The conditions were typical English but Shastri came out with flying colors. He also scored a ton against the West Indians quicks in their own backyard. For the record, he batted at each and every position!

In the 1985 World Championship of Cricket, which

India handsomely won, Shastri was named 'Champion of Champions' and presented with an Audi. Shastri's mantra in life is simple: do what you enjoy; only then can you perform to the best of your abilities. His teammates endorse this notion. A brilliant reader of the game, Shastri was also looked up to as someone who could lead India. Alas, he led India in just one Test, and won it. A man who would speak his mind on the field, he hung up his boots in 1992 at the age of 30. Nowadays, he speaks his mind as a television commentator.

Strangely enough, people forget Shastri's captaincy. Curiously enough, it was Kapil who seldom enjoyed the burden of captaincy. Kapil and Shastri were both great all-rounders. They gave everything they could. India had always craved for a genuine all-rounder and, all of a sudden, we found two. Shastri was a stubborn batsman and a persevering bowler. Kapil, on the other hand, was a lethal fast bowler and India's first. And that courage showed in his flamboyant batting.

Sachin Tendulkar

Virender Sehwag

Cricket might have a lot to do with technique, style and skill. But it's a spectator sport. Players play for the gallery. Some cricketers ignore this basic fact. They are obsessed with the technicalities of the game. Some play for records, others play for the team. But there are some who play for the millions who adore them.

Fans pin their hopes on this brand of cricketers. How does an Indian win affect a fan's life, you'd wonder. Does his income swell? Or does it fetch him a new house? These fans find happiness through their cricketers.

Sachin Tendulkar and Virender Sehwag have been spreading happiness for years together. Whatever be the format, their mission is to hit the ball all over the park as frequently as possible. And when they succeed, so do their fans.

At 40, Tendulkar changed. He didn't play with the sole intention of taking the bowlers to the cleaners. He took his time before toying with them. On the other hand, Sehwag is essentially himself. He is as much himself now, as he ever was and perhaps will be. Form or lack of it, the Sehwag brand of cricket is immutable.

And yet, Sehwag manages to surprise and shock the best of bowlers time and again. Never formally coached, it is his street smart attitude that makes him a great batsman. His street-smartness comes from years of tennis-ball cricket played in the by-lanes of Najafgarh in the outskirts of Delhi. He has the uncanny knack of gauging the pace of the pitch which is so essential for an opener.

At the international level, bowlers come to the ground with a comprehensive plan for every batsman. Sehwag's brilliance lies in the accuracy with which he senses their instincts and reads their moves. While bowlers and captains sweat over important facets like setting the field, Sehwag's God-sent gift – his hand-eye coordination, reverses all.

Once while playing for Leicestershire, Sehwag and his partner were all at sea against a fast bowler who was reversing the ball at great speed. The ball was coming at an impossible angle. Sehwag came out with his own plan. "Let's lose the ball", he said.

Viru's partner did not get head or tail of what he'd said. Sehwag explained, "Look, if we hit the ball out of the ground and onto the road, that ball can't be retrieved. The bowler has worked on the shine of the ball and that's why he's getting to reverse it at will. If we 'lose' the ball, he will have to work all over again on the new ball. We can score easily!"

His partner couldn't believe what he'd heard. Moments later, Sehwag tonked the ball and it travelled some distance. The operative part is that he had 'lost' it. Mission accomplished, you see. It is through such uncomplicated and innocent means that Sehwag ruled. He called the shots, literally.

Tendulkar had his own street-smart theories. Growing up, he was one of the many thousand kids in Mumbai for whom playing cricket was an indispensable part of life. In those narrow alleys crowded with scooters and carts, the word 'boundary' has a different meaning. Hitting beyond this scooter will fetch you "2D"; placing it anywhere before the vehicle "1D". "D" stands for declared. Smash the headlights and you are out. You'd also have to deal with the owner of the vehicle.

Mumbai's railway stations are dotted with schoolboys burdened with backpacks double their size. They play 'shots' in imitation of their heroes. Missing homework is OK; bunking practice is not.

Sachin Tendulkar was just 12 when his coach, Ramakant Achrekar, wanted him to be selected for the Shatkar Trophy, a selection trial tournament for the Under-19s. In his second match, Tendulkar scored a century, the knock studded with some brilliant shots. Sachin Ramesh Tendulkar had taken very few years to arrive. He was 'there' even in 1985. In spite of excelling in the tournament, he was picked only for the Under-15 Mumbai team. The selectors felt he was too young to play Under-19 cricket. Four years later, he would play his Test debut against Pakistan!

In the season following his rejection, Tendulkar amassed more than 2,000 runs in junior tournaments for his school and state. And when he wasn't given the Mumbai Cricket Association's 'Best Junior Cricketer' award, he wept bitterly. Was he really too young then? Sunil Gavaskar saw something in the boy.

In a handwritten letter dated August 1987, the 'Little Master' wrote, *"Dear Sachin, I wanted to write earlier, but something or the other came in the way. Then I thought it better to write at the beginning of the new season rather than at the end of last season. Congratulations on your performance last season. What was most impressive was the way you batted alone when the others around you were not contributing much. Keep it up. Also please do not neglect your studies. My experience is that education helps you through bad patches in whichever career you choose.*

So go ahead and God bless.
Regards,
Sunil Gavaskar
PS: Don't be disappointed at not getting the Best Junior Cricketer award from the BCA. If you look at the best award winners, you will find one name missing and that person has not done too badly in Test cricket!!"

Tendulkar wasn't too young. In fact for his age and size, he was brave. Playing a senior tournament for the MIG Cricket Club as a 12-year-old, Tendulkar's partner remembers a ball going right past the boy's right eye. Senior pro Satish Samant walked down to him and said, "You were lucky. Your right eye would have gone with the ball." The little chap replied, "But had I connected, it would have gone for a six." The very next ball, Tendulkar sent the ball soaring out of the ground and followed it up with four more shots to the boundary.

Talk about hitting the ball indiscriminately to the boundary, and one has to mention Sehwag. In fact, Sehwag was included in the Under-19 team as an off-spinner who could bat in the middle order. His reflexes were amazing and skipper Ganguly envisaged him as an opener. Ganguly's decision was under scrutiny and if the move hadn't clicked, he would have been severely criticized.

Sehwag is indeed a strange player. A player who describes his job as just "going out there and hitting the ball", he has scored two triple hundreds and a 293 in Test cricket. During the Lahore Test in 2006, he treated Pakistan bowlers with disdain. His opening stand with Rahul Dravid is the stuff of legends. They fell just three runs short of the age-old record (413) set by Vinoo Mankad and Pankaj Roy. An innocent Sehwag didn't know of the legends or their feat! There was no malice, mind you. It's just that he was never a 'history' man. Numbers never mattered to him. He played in the moment; he played for the moment. And he played to score runs.

Sehwag was not a prodigy like Tendulkar. He did not take the cricketing world by storm. But Sehwag was special. He thrived under pressure. A non-regular opener, his is an unbelievable success story. Perhaps, it has a lot to do with the faith Ganguly had in him. As VVS Laxman puts it, "Viru was a special player. He was an impact player and always gave the team the momentum. It was good batting with him as it took away the pressure off me. He has always been an instinctive player and his eye-hand co-ordination was very good. The greatness of Viru was that he could score runs even off good deliveries and put pressure on the bowlers."

Whenever Sehwag and Tendulkar played together, they matched each other stroke for stroke. Watching Sehwag made people revisit Tendulkar's early days. As a youngster, Tendulkar, too, was brutally attacking. But he always remained grounded and committed to the cause of the team.

Not many were surprised when Sachin scored a century on his first-class debut. A couple of days earlier, he had scored a big hundred in school cricket. Tendulkar's Mumbai debut was just another school game for him. The team comprised seniors like Dilip Vengsarkar, who had played for the country for over a decade, but Sachin did not feel conscious. The confidence he displayed was impeccable. He was neither smug nor insecure.

It is very difficult to pen anything on the effect Tendulkar has had on Indian cricket. Anything and everything you say about him is, well, clichéd.

There also came a time when he struggled with a nasty tennis elbow. The God of cricket was frustrated to no end. Not being able to touch the bat was the biggest punishment for him. But he managed to put his head down and bide his time. He emerged from this difficult phase by remaining focused and positive.

The result: his game became a tad tighter. He seldom played those expansive drives; instead, he chose to caress the ball through the gaps. Thanks to the injury, Tendulkar added one more feather to his artistic cap. Enormous control and economy of movement began to redefine Sachin.

As Amol Muzumdar says, "Maturity was apparent in Sachin's game right from his early teens. Twenty years down the line, it is still there. Now, he sets specific goals for himself. Apart from the lofty ideals of playing for the country and winning matches, he has the individual drive to look perfect and classy."

But there are people who would rather watch the older version of Tendulkar. Kapil Dev has this to say in 2012: "All the great attacking batsmen never changed their style. Sir Garfield Sobers, Sir Vivian Richards, Brian Lara and many others played attacking cricket all their life, but Tendulkar altered his game after his tennis elbow injury. He started batting like Sunil Gavaskar who, after scoring a century, would take a single off the next ball and then again take time to plan another hundred. People feel he should quit the game mainly because they are not used to watching him bat slow. But who are we to talk about his retirement? It's his call and if he is not performing, it's the call of the selectors."

So what does it feel to be like Sachin Tendulkar? Everybody wants to know this. What goes through his mind when he sees people holding posters that read, 'CRICKET IS OUR RELIGION, SACHIN IS OUR GOD'!

Unlike Sehwag, Tendulkar doesn't exactly enjoy pressure. At the same time, he doesn't get consumed by pressure. Till his injury in 2006, he never gave the impression that he felt any pressure. On his return, he displayed the same kind of vigour. He only altered his batting manual.

Laxman has had many partnerships with Tendulkar. He has been blessed to see Tendulkar play from the best seat in the stadium – the non-striker's end. "I made my Test debut under his captaincy in 1996. He is one of the calmest people around. He had an amazing knack of assessing the situation and reacting accordingly. He always had the talent and also the mental strength to respond to any challenge. It was a pleasure playing alongside him. That knock against Australia in Sharjah, which took India into the final of the 1998 tri-series, was a treat to watch from the best place on the ground. It was complete domination. His 241-run knock in Sydney in 2004 was a treat of a different kind in the sense that he resisted the cover drive and yet scored those runs. It was an amazing exhibition of mental strength."

Laxman goes on. "Sachin's USP remains his mental strength. Or should we say mental discipline? He would envision situations many days prior to the start of a series and practise (practice) accordingly. Before the Australians landed in India in 1998, he was well-armed to handle Shane Warne who the Australians deemed would be deadly on the slow turners of India. And given that spin was our strength (it still is!), the pitches were prepared accordingly. Warne could have wreaked havoc."

Here's what Tendulkar did. He summoned all the leg spinners in Mumbai and had them bowl to him in the rough he had created around the leg stump. At the MIG Cricket Club, he employed the sweep shot to anything that was pitched in the rough. The bowlers weren't even state-level, but the objective was to get used to the angle. One club-level bowler said Tendulkar was beaten just once during the whole exercise. And believe it or not, it was a 12-year-old who'd foxed him!

And when Warne had the ball, cricket lovers the world over waited with bated breath. He enticed Tendulkar with a top-spinner pitched on leg, quietly hoping that the revolutions on the ball would make him mistime it. But the more Warne bowled those deliveries, the more frequently he was dispatched to the square-leg boundary. That innings set the tone for the series. Later, we would also see Navjot Singh Sidhu dance down the wicket to loft Warne over his head. Tendulkar would, of course, mercilessly sweep Warne. The preparations had paid off.

The late Peter Roebuck, former Somerset captain and one of the finest cricket writers ever, was a big fan of Tendulkar. In Sach – Genius Unplugged, he wrote, "Tendulkar does not seek to announce or shrivel or buoy himself or turn a park into a battleground. It is enough for him that cricket is a game, his favourite game. He does not need anything else. Always it has been the same. The most underestimated thing about him is his longevity, his steadiness. Throughout twenty years of intense pressure and unrelenting exposure, he has retained his delight. Through it all, he has managed to focus on the next ball and the next innings. There have been no demons. Remaining simple is difficult and he has managed it. By no means is it the least of his contributions."

Roebuck was fortunate enough to play with Richards for Somerset. His comparison of the two greats is thus highly useful, "Richards nurtured majesty; Tendulkar leans towards the common man. Except that excitement builds around the ground as his name is put on the board, it might be another man emerging through the gate. Richards and Tendulkar also used to bat differently. In Richards's hand it was not a tool but a weapon. The niceties were not for him. To compare Richards's batting with Tendulkar's is to put culture against a civilisation."

He goes on, "Tendulkar is a purist, in command of himself even amidst a withering attack, contemplatively yet rarely hesitant, stylish yet not giving style more than it is due. He can concentrate without apparent effort and so does not need to summon any dark force to urge him along. Batting is part of his essence."

Roebuck and I would often take a walk after the end of the day's play. Walking through the sprawling maidan of

Esplanade in Kolkata, we would often discuss Tendulkar. He had heard and read a lot about Tendulkar's heroics. After playing a lot with Richards and watching a lot of Tendulkar, Roebuck was candid enough to say that Tendulkar played for the team. The Mumbaikar, he said, would change gears as per the situation. On the other hand, Richards was always keen to show that he was the boss.

Greg Chappell, who coached India, is all praise for Tendulkar's mental strength and batsmanship. "The most gifted batsmen that I have seen are, in chronological order, Neil Harvey, Garfield Sobers, Graeme Pollock, Doug Walters, Barry Richards, Viv Richards, Sachin Tendulkar, Brian Lara and Ricky Ponting. Each of them had the ability to dramatically alter the course of a game that differentiates them from other outstanding batsmen of their time.

"It is hard to imagine that Tendulkar first played Test cricket at the tender age of 16. That he played for 24 years is astonishing, because I believe everyone has a finite number of significant performances in them. To think that he has carried the hopes and expectations of more than a billion people each time he batted set him apart, even from Donald Bradman.

"He also played in many more countries and varied conditions than Bradman. Along the way, he compiled a batting record that may never be challenged. This can be credited to an awesome talent, a unique grounding and an ability to switch off from the distractions around him.

"I had the privilege of working with Sachin closely for about two years. In that time, I saw a side of him that few people would have seen. I saw the sublime artist with bat in hand; I saw the little boy that he once was; I saw his vulnerability, and I saw a man who had to compartmentalize himself in a way that would have tested a lesser individual.

"In December 2005, we were in Chennai and I was in my room at the Taj after we had trained at Chepauk. My phone rang and it was Sachin asking if he could come over and have a chat about his batting. I agreed and he came over immediately. We talked for a few hours during which he bared his soul in a manner that I believe was rare for him. He showed a hint of vulnerability that I doubt many had seen. He asked about why batting got more difficult as one got older.

"At the end of our discussion, he thanked me and as he was leaving, I commented on how difficult it must be for him to keep up with his many friends around India. I had seen people coming and going from his room, so I assumed that some of them were friends. He looked at me momentarily before saying, 'Greg, you have more friends in India than I have'. I got the shock of my life and at that moment I realized how tough it was being Sachin Tendulkar.

"It may explain why he survived for so long and why he was so good; batting was what he lived for. It was the way that he defined himself. As with Bradman, Sachin's brilliance can largely be put down to his early experiences. In Sachin's case, he was allowed to bat in multiple games. Once dismissed in a game, his coach was known to take him to another, to arrange for him to bat again. This variety of experiences against different opposition under diverse conditions allowed him to hone his decision-making, as much as his method. Without this grounding, I doubt that he could have reached such heights so early, or maintained such a high level of performance for so long. Indian cricket may never see an individual with such an incredible combination of mental and physical skills.

"True, to remain focused for more than two decades and not get into any controversy is something that speaks about his character. Season after season, he has worked on his technique. One gets the impression that not only does he work on his technique but he also works on his fitness. He sets personal goals and goes about achieving it quite systematically."

Focus, sincerity and dedication – Tendulkar wasn't born with these virtues. Virender Sehwag was the antithesis of Sachin. A genius, he did not use all his talent. In fact, Sehwag's attitude left the likes of Chappell frustrated.

Here's what Chappell has to say about Viru. "In fact, Sehwag is the most gifted ball striker that I have seen. I remember the first time I was able to watch him closely. It was in Bangalore soon after I took over as the national coach. Viru arrived early for a camp at a time when 30 of the best pace bowlers from around India were finishing off a camp of their own. He asked if he could have a hit against some of them in a center wicket session.

"We were on the National Cricket Academy ground which is wedged in the triangle formed by the confluence of Cubbon and Queen Roads to the side of the M Chinnaswamy Stadium. The wicket was well-grassed and bouncy, but he walked in with a new bat and hit everything sweetly from the middle.

"Considering the wicket and that the bowlers were swinging, seaming and bouncing the ball disconcertingly, this was as awesome a display of menacing power and precision batting as I had witnessed. I was excited about working with someone with such sublime skill.

"To say that Viru was one of the great frustrations of my time with the team is an understatement. Sadly, he continues to disappoint and is in danger of squandering his God-given talent. But the person who is least likely to be fazed by all of this is Virender himself.

"What I soon learned about him was that Viru did not want to dedicate himself to taking his talent to its zenith. He was happy to turn up and play and accept what came his way. No amount of cajoling from me could shift him from his insouciant way.

This often happens to those with the greatest gift. Because he had never had to work hard at developing such a skill, Viru did not know how to dedicate himself to disciplined training. It was only during periods of relatively poor form that he was prepared to spend time getting things back on track. As soon as he made some runs, he slipped back into old habits and appeared content to practice in the same old profligate way until his form evaporated again.

"His idea of a practice session was to hit the bowlers as hard and as far as he could as often as he could. Most balls were hit in the air with no regard to whether or not they were out. I tried to encourage him to work on developing his range by playing each ball on its merit and developing some power shots on the leg side against pace.

"Because Viru was so strong on the off side and only wanted to play on that side of the wicket, teams bowled very straight to him to deny him room to free his arms. I tried to explain to him that if he was prepared to work on developing leg side options against the faster bowlers, it would, in fact, force them to bowl more to his strength. He wasn't interested.

"The other area of frustration for me was that he did not keep himself in good shape and would often be troubled by a back ailment that restricted him in the field and made him even less likely to want to put time into expanding his ability. Apart from his batting skills, he is a very talented off-spin bowler and he should have been the best slip fielder in the team, but he eschewed the responsibility at every opportunity.

"Strangely, for someone who only wants to play the game on his terms, he harbours a desire to captain his country. I have no doubt that he could do it for he understands the game well, but what he fails to grasp is that with the honor comes responsibility. In fact, the responsibility to show personal leadership has to come before one can earn the higher honor. He wants the prize, but has been unwilling to pay the price."

Chappell's frustration is understandable. But given that Sehwag is happy with whatever he gets, it only adds to his charm. He is not there to prove anything to anyone. Records fail to motivate him. Sehwag plays because he likes to and for the people who like to watch him play.

Tendulkar, too, has been burdened with expectations. But despite the hoopla around him, Tendulkar managed to enjoy his game. He and Sehwag have made the cricket lover an intrinsic part of the game. Not only have they taken the sport to the viewer but they have also brought the viewer to the sport.

Rahul Dravid

VVS Laxman

Eden Gardens. Few places in the world can do to you what Eden Gardens can. What makes this venue remarkable is that no instant images of fierce matches come to mind first up. It is not through hoopla or controversy that the Eden is special. The stadium captivates the imagination of cricket itself; it makes one think about cricket. Nothing else.

The Eden is one arena where India need not be in a winning position, and the match will still be appreciated. There have been times when the result would be a foregone conclusion before the start of play on Day Five, but the stands would still be packed. Is it Kolkata's sporting spirit? Or is it the city's undying belief in miracles? We do not know. But they always turn up in huge numbers.

Eden: The Arena

If football has its Old Traffords and Anfields, San Siros and Bernebeaus, Maracanas and Mineirãos, cricket has the Eden. That's all it needs, really.

The footpaths of Chowrangee Street, Park Street, the buses, the trams – all these bring Kolkata to life on the day of a match. To add to the spectacle are the mounted policemen, trying to caution the fans from the comfort of their saddle. But the crowd loves cricket too much to care.

Apart from the unfortunate – and surprising – crowd trouble in 1966 against the West Indies and during the 1996 World Cup semifinal, the Eden fans have always been among the best in the world. So welcoming and so intimate is the setting that every player just loves playing here. The year 1972 saw us journalists in the press box forget our jobs and join the crowd in bellowing "Bowwwwlllled" as BS Chandrashekhar started his run up.

So, when in 2000-2001, Steve Waugh and his ferocious gang landed in Kolkata after thrashing India in Mumbai by 10 wickets, the City of Joy was still at its enthusiastic best. Australia had just recorded their 16th consecutive Test victory. They were virtually steamrollering teams. Surface, weather, conditions – these variables never bothered them. Every player in that team was lethal.

When the grand Australian team arrived in Eden for a practice session two days prior to the start of the Test, a policeman on duty excitedly applauded them. It was the visitors everybody wanted to see. That's all they cared about. India just happened to be Australia's next 'target', the means for them to etch another massive world record. No one gave Sourav Ganguly & Co. a semblance of a chance. Not too long ago, the match-fixing controversy had ravaged cricket in the country. India had a new man at the helm. Could he even make for a decent captain?

The Match That's Never Found a Match

The Australians went about their task in commanding fashion, piling up 445 after winning the toss. By the evening of the second day, the writing was on the wall. India had slipped to 128 for eight. Waugh's boys were simply ruthless. And not for the first time, India's famed batting line-up resembled a bunch of gawky schoolboys. The bowlers were bowling to the field and the slip cordon was ready to pouch anything that came its way.

Cricket has witnessed many a champion side over the centuries, but three of those squads stand out. Bradman's Invincibles of the late 1940s, Lloyd's (later Richards's) Unmatchables of the 1970s and 1980s and Waugh's (later Ponting's) Unbeatables of the 1990s and early 2000s were simply peerless. This is just to give you an idea about the challenge the Indians, a side in transition were faced with. It was David vs Goliath. Nothing less.

India put up a brief resistance on Day Three before folding up for 171. Of course, the crowd wasn't expecting India to thrash Australia. However, this kind of humiliation was beyond imagination. When Waugh enforced the follow-on, the spectators bit their nails anticipating another embarrassing Indian defeat. One wondered if India could at least avoid an innings defeat.

But what unraveled in front of our eyes that day was beyond the imagination of even the most optimistic of Indian fans. The first innings had seen one Indian batsman tease his mates by showing off his stylistics. The others were merely worried about guarding their stumps. The man in question had tackled the bowling quite easily. There was no fuss. He showed no haste in dealing with the thunderbolts of Glenn McGrath and Jason Gillespie. And he patiently dealt with the revolutions Shane Warne imparted on the ball. Not to mention the turn and bounce offered by the wicket.

The Great Indian Fightback

This is why VVS Laxman was promoted to No. 3 in the next innings on that fateful day. He would, at least, delay the inevitable. India had six wickets left to see them through two days – a laughable situation.

Fans coated with too many layers of hope quoted the 1966 Test between England and the West Indies at Lord's, London. The visitors were in dire straits when they lost half their side by lunch on Day Four. But the great Sir Garfield Sobers and his cousin, David Holford, batted till the end of the fifth day to force a draw.

But how often do these things happen? Here was Ganguly, consumed by the combination of Gilchrist-McGrath while India were four down for 232 and still 39 away from making Australia bat again. With the deficit now looking manageable, the unthinkable was starting to gain thought in some people's minds. Dravid, the huge wall of Indian cricket, was there alright, but what could have he done alone? Who would keep him company? At the end of Day Three, India were four down for 254 with Laxman batting on 109 and Dravid on 7. No one had any inkling about the drama that was to unfold on Day Four.

At stumps, Australians were probably dreaming of their 17th consecutive Test win. Not to forget the series. They didn't know that the next day would turn out to be a nightmare beyond measure.

Day Four of the 2001 Eden Gardens Test will go down in the annals of cricket as one of the finest rearguard actions ever recorded by two Indian batsmen. Dravid and

Laxman teased and tormented the Aussie attack to such an extent that it seemed unreal. Waugh looked clueless after lunch. Perhaps, for the first time in 17 Tests, his authority was being challenged.

Laxman and Dravid had done something few Indians could imagine, leave alone achieve. They had turned the tables on the opposition, putting them in a pressure cooker situation. Their resolve mirrored the atmosphere at the Eden. As a noted journalist sitting next to me in the press box wrote, "The atmosphere on the ground is making them enjoy every moment of it and when that happens, the lovely game of cricket looks a different ball game".

Laxman was short-circuiting Warne's moves by effortlessly playing him. Yes, there was an element of risk in some of his shots, but when luck favours you, why bother! Dravid, on the other hand, was his usual self. He was a wall. Defending like his life depended on it, he was concentration personified. That, however, didn't stop him from playing the occasional majestic stroke. Laxman and Dravid seamlessly complemented each other. The day ended with the scoreboard reading four down for 584, Laxman was batting on 275 and Dravid 155. That day had seen them bat 90 overs for the addition of 335 runs! The Australians were faced with a kind of pressure they seldom had. They could not handle it. They had to save face. And on Day Five, the unthinkable actually happened. India won the Test handsomely.

What Laxman and Dravid together did at the Eden was a perfect representation of both their careers. The character they displayed that day was visible in both of them from the very beginning. And by beginning, I mean their formative years, more specifically their Under-19 days. Laxman's batting, his walk and other mannerisms pleasantly resembled Mohammad Azharuddin's and yet had its unique charm. There were many other Hyderabadis trying to imitate Azhar, but Laxman absorbed Azhar's style rather nicely. His flicks had the same patent. He had the uncanny knack of piercing the gaps in the field.

Laxman always took a special liking for the Australians. And he was at his very best when he took on them in their own backyard. Those pitches Down Under offered consistent bounce. They helped his style of playing on the up. His knock of 167 at Sydney in 1999, was full of front-foot drives; each of them carried a stamp of class. He pulled the ball with such disdain that the Australian fast bowlers couldn't believe their fate. It was more like the treatment meted out to them by their own batsmen at the nets! The more they bounced Laxman, the faster the ball disappeared. Attempted Yorkers were dealt with delectable glides and leg-glances. And when faced with a rising ball just short of length, Laxman would get on the back foot and caress it through the covers, leaving the best of fielders stunned.

Born and brought up in the Garden City, Dravid had played his cricket on coir mats. Batsmen from Karnataka were predominantly stroke players. GR Viswanath and Brijesh Patel had the potential to shred any attack to pieces. Dravid watched a lot of such stroke players, but even as a teenager he never indulged in an exaggerated display of stroke play. He believed in staying put. But when a loose

ball came along, he played his shots.

Youngsters must imbibe this very quality of Dravid. You are to play to your strengths. You are to play for your team, not the gallery. Dravid never got carried away. He could have easily aped the legends he watched growing up. But he didn't. Instead, he chose to focus on his own inimitable style. And look where he's now: greater than GRV, greater than SMG. And to some, greater even than Sachin Ramesh Tendulkar. The important thing, then, is to stick to your style. There's a different high in watching others following in your footsteps. And I know of many youngsters who want to become 'The Next Wall'.

Sandeep Patil first watched Laxman as coach of the India Under-19 side touring England. "Cricket has some good artists and a few great artists. I was lucky to have either played with or watched them. To me, Vishy, Azhar and 'Very Very Special' Laxman are great artists. You don't describe them. You just watch them perform with utmost ease. In white flannels, VVS was a giant." During the course of the tour, Patil knew he had witnessed something special.

Laxman: A Visual Treat

Besides being a visual Treat, Laxman was very useful in the batting line-up as he helped pace the innings. It was an important role because he batted at No. 6 most of the time. This is what Laxman has to say about his role. "Pacing one's innings is very important. But at the same time, it is equally important to cash in on loose deliveries early on in your innings. And that means one can't be over-cautious. I always paced my innings according to the conditions, bowlers and the situation. As I went along, my range of strokes opened up and the runs came. At times, I had to play certain bowlers differently and that also played a part in pacing my innings".

Though both were the official iron rods of the Indian team, always dependable and sturdy, Dravid and Laxman had contrasting styles. Laxman would get excited at scoring opportunities and pounce on them like a tiger on its prey. Dravid, however, was ultra-reserved. The IPL has, perhaps, shown us that Dravid can play any stroke. But during his time with the Indian team, he realized he was the cushion that the whole team was banking on. And that's why he made 'caution' his second name.

With Sehwag opening the innings, there was always the possibility of India losing a wicket early. Batting at No. 3, Dravid had to be padded up the moment the openers left the pavilion. Well, there were occasions when he walked out to face the 200th ball of the innings, but mind you, Dravid would be mentally prepared even before the first ball was to be bowled.

He was aware of the risks facing his team. However, when conditions suited batting and bowlers faltered in line and length, he would display his beautiful cover drive or on-drive. Having played his early cricket on matting wickets, he preferred to be on the back foot. But exposure to turf cricket helped him become a good front-foot player too. He missed a hundred on debut, at Lord's, by just five runs but that innings is etched in the memory of many, including that of Peter May.

Greg Chappell reiterates his appreciation of Dravid. "He will make a brilliant ICC chairman in 10 years' time. The BCCI and the ICC must find a way of getting him involved. He is a man who commands instant respect, not just because of his stirring deeds on the cricket field but because of his sharp intellect and broad vision. He is probably the best-read cricketer in the game and has genuine intellectual curiosity. The game will go on without Rahul Dravid. Other players with talent will be found, but the question is, will they be able to find one person with the talent, courage, integrity and insatiable drive to keep improving himself as Dravid did? To me, Rahul's career embodied the words of Mahatma Gandhi who said that in a gentle way, you can shake the world."

If this isn't a mighty compliment, then what is? And mind you Chappell isn't easy to impress. That's Dravid for you. His dignity commands respect, nay reverence. And that's how we must all strive to be. After all, don't we all want to be loved and adored? There's no fun in just excelling at what you do. You've got to inspire people around you. And to do that, you must shower love.

The grand Indian batting line-up with Dravid at No. 3, Tendulkar at four and Ganguly at five looked formidable. It was on the other hand unfortunate that Laxman had to bat at six. However, it's a crucial position in Test cricket as the No. 6 batsman, invariably, faces the second new ball. While the role of the openers is to see the shine off the new ball, the No. 6 batsman has to attack the fast bowlers who could be into their third spell.

At No. 6, Laxman was also faced with crises. There are times when the team loses four wickets for 100 or less in a Test match and with not much batting to come; the No. 6 has to take complete charge. Needless to say, Laxman did this admirably. Not only did he offer an impeccably straight bat, he made India win Test matches from losing positions while batting with tail-enders like Pragyan Ojha and Ishant Sharma. While the opposition attacked relentlessly sensing victory, Laxman would protect the tail without taking his eye off the larger goal – victory. He was the perfect example of someone who did not lose track of the target.

Dravid and Laxman share a special connection. Speaking about Dravid's batting, Laxman says, "Rahul and I have always batted well together as we played a lot of junior and first-class cricket together. Rahul looked very comfortable at international level right from the start of his career. He always gave a lot of importance to technique and because of that he was very successful wherever he played. His work ethic is exemplary. The partnership in Kolkata was one of the best we had. The team needed it the most and we had to get out of a difficult situation. Also, the series was on the line. We could not think too far ahead of ourselves so we kept supporting each other and took each ball as it came. It was draining, both physically and mentally. Rahul showed how strong he is mentally and fought it out to play a match-winning knock".

It must not be forgotten that besides the burden of being the team's anchor, Dravid had to put up with the task of keeping wickets for much of his career. Not many know that Dravid was, in fact, forced to keep wickets on his first tour to England. Nayan Mongia was the sole wicketkeeper and Sanjay Manjrekar was foolishly named as Mongia's substitute.

Dravid was given the extra job, rather unceremoniously. In fact, he hadn't even carried his wicket-keeping gloves to England! But when it is your debut series, players generally obey the team management. Later in his career, in order to get the balance of the team right, Ganguly and the selectors made Dravid keep wickets in ODIs. Hence, Dravid was forced to bear the extra burden. Alas, he was prone to developing swollen palms because he wasn't well-versed with the nuances of wicket-keeping. The pressure of wicket-keeping in limited-overs cricket was enormous because a dropped catch could cost the game and invite much criticism.

Now that's a team man right there. A shining example, so to speak. Always remember that cricket is a team game played by individuals. Some do try and become greater than the game itself. But they eventually perish. Stalwarts like Dravid, Laxman and Tendulkar respect the game more than anything else. For, they know that the game always rewards you. Try and 'shortchange' the game, and you will pay the price.

While Dravid was busy carrying the load of the Indian team on his shoulders, the selectors were developing cold feet. They felt he was "too slow" and cited his "poor" strike rate. The 1998 season proved terrible for him as the so called wise men weren't impressed with just his technical preciseness. In ODI cricket, batsmen have to step up while facing bowlers of Test quality. Dravid wasn't the kind to bicker. He humbly thought, "May be I needed to improve. I was forced to improve."

Forever the team man, he chose to adopt rather than complain. Any budding cricketer must know this: the game is forever changing. There was a time when scoring 300 in an ODI was unthinkable. Today, 350 is the norm! How, then, does one rise to the challenge. Well, you've got to go back to the basics, adopt and evolve. Dravid, like all great players, did just that. And the results paint a pretty picture.

Dravid's mere presence blunted the most brutal of attacks. He would rotate the strike against the razor-sharp bowling units of Pakistan and South Africa, a role Ravi Shastri essayed as an opener in Australia in 1985.

However, the selectors seemed to have developed new ideas of how an ODI player should be. After burdening him with umpteen responsibilities for years together, they said the Indian team needed a natural player, not a cautious one.

However, the strength that Dravid offered couldn't be wished away too easily and he came back strongly to lead the team in the 2007 World Cup. Captaincy, however, turned out to be a nightmare for the cool and calculative Dravid. He was methodical, could handle the pressure and stay firm. Why then, one might wonder, did Dravid not click as a captain?

Was Chappell's larger-than-life presence too much for Dravid to handle? Was it too much for the skipper to assert his authority? There is a school of thought that feels

Dravid was conscious of the circumstances under which he replaced Ganguly. It was that ugly spat between Chappell and Ganguly that led to the latter's downfall. But if you analyze the events, Dravid exercised his right as a captain to do what he felt was right.

During the course of the series in Pakistan, in 2006, we got to see a glimpse of Dravid the leader. He opted to open the innings with Sehwag in the Lahore Test. The cricketing world watched the on-field drama, with Ganguly questioning Dravid and Chappell listening patiently. It was a clear case of Dravid asserting himself as captain. He had done the same when Tendulkar was on 194 in Multan, in 2004. As always, Dravid made it a point to show that he was the boss.

Sometimes, just sometimes, a leader has to take tough calls. You'd think you don't want to invite the ire of your teammates. But there are instances when, as captain, you just have to take unpopular decisions. Declaring the innings close in Multan and denying Tendulkar the chance of registering a double hundred was one such controversial decision Dravid made. He didn't obviously make new fans, but the important thing is he stood by his call. Almost a decade later, you'd think he was right.

The Reluctant Hero

Says Chappell, "Rahul appeared to me to be a reluctant hero. He preferred to be left alone to play cricket and was not bothered about the trappings and demands of success.

He was, in fact, one of a kind. He has truly done India proud. Dravid was indisputably one of the gentlemen of the game which he has adorned for over 15 years. Not for him the tantrums of the superstar, just quiet dedication to a task that he so obviously loved. Very few have ever played the game in a better spirit. The game will be poorer without his sporting ways."

While Dravid was juggling his roles of Mr Responsible Batsman and Mr Wicketkeeper, Laxman's natural style, too, was being tinkered with. Watching him thrash international bowlers with disdain, the selectors asked him to open the innings. As a former India opener, a shrewd thinker of the game and someone who has watched Laxman since his formative days, ML Jaisimha said, "I am happy he wasn't over-coached. Most of the Hyderabadi players are natural. They have their own style. Yes, at times, they struggle but, more often than not, their attacking style enables them to find a way out. Azharuddin and Laxman, both wristy players, played shots that may have looked risky to you and me. But they were confident of pulling it off. And that's when you should not tell them to curb their stroke play."

Laxman and Dravid drew the line between being technically sound and slaves of technique. They made sure they played cricket and not the other way round. Being technically correct, they sometimes gave way to instinct and opened up, just like GR Viswanath. It's not that Dravid didn't have the guts to play his shots. But the lessons of 1998 prompted him to be safe. He never took his place for granted.

They say form is temporary, class is permanent. It's important that one stays grounded. Look how Dravid valued his place in the team. If a certain mistake leads to your downfall, you just don't repeat it. That's exactly what Dravid did – he deleted his past and looked at the future.

Rising to the Occasion

The way he played with youngsters Mohammad Kaif and Yuvraj Singh in the NatWest final, guiding them and yet batting beautifully showed he had a lot to offer to the team. Be it a Test or an ODI, Dravid always made sure he paced the innings. Some would say he ought to have taken a little more risk in limited-overs cricket. But it is perhaps in blue clothing, when the entire team thinks it is compelled to blast bowlers, that you need an anchor like Dravid. Moreover, when the situation demanded, Dravid stamped his class. The game against South Africa was an eye-opener to the selectors who were looking for an excuse to drop him.

The Proteas made 279, a formidable score given that the hosts had a bowling attack comprising Allan Donald, Shaun Pollock, Lance Klusener, Jacques Kallis and skipper Hansie Cronje. After the rains, the D/L Method reduced the target to 251 in 40 overs. Dravid seized the day by whacking the famed bowlers all over the park. When faced by a quick delivery, he went on the front foot and hit White Lightning over the sightscreen for a six. He scored 84 with five fours and one six in just 94 deliveries.

Unlucky Laxman

It is ironical that, in spite of being a stroke player, Laxman played just 86 ODIs. Dravid appeared in 344. It would seem that for a natural player like Laxman, limited-overs cricket would be the apt field but it wasn't. A huge setback to Laxman's chances in the ODI team was his fielding. His batting might have had the spark of Azharuddin, but his fielding certainly didn't. While Azhar was electrifying in the field, Laxman was slow to say the least. Being a specialist slip fielder he didn't make an effort to work on sprints. Even if Laxman had half the fielding genius that Azharuddin had, he could have never been dropped from the team.

It wasn't Laxman's inconsistency or lack of performance that led to his exclusion from the ODI team. Laxman says, "I was indeed disappointed when I was not selected for some series and matches. When you are representing the country, you always want to play. Getting dropped for the 2003 World Cup was a big disappointment because I had a very consistent run in the lead up to the tournament and more specifically the ODI series against the West Indies in India".

Both Dravid and Laxman were victims of the "new age" of Indian cricket. They were told they were too slow, that they need to change themselves to survive. What spectators and selectors alike did not notice that it was in fact because of lion-hearted players like Dravid and Laxman that the rest of the team could act frivolous and 'brave'. Always dependable, they offered the base, the spring for the new age Team India to surface.

The two legendary partnerships of Laxman and Dravid against Australia in Kolkata (2001) and Adelaide (2003) speak volumes, almost epitomizing their characters. They were men of partnerships, men of stability. And more than anything else, they were certainly men of honor.

Mahendra Singh Dhoni

Virat Kohli

Leaders are often not born; rather they are made. The living proofs of this are the present-day champions Mahendra Singh Dhoni and Virat Kohli. While the former, besides bringing glory to the country, has brought his simple hometown into the limelight of the cricketing world. The other is a promising leader of the future cricket of India.

West Bengal's Kharagpur station boasts of the longest platform in the world. However, to a man entrusted with the job of checking tickets, this 'did you know?' fact didn't really matter. His job was mundane to say the least. He was nevertheless, happy. Did he predict that life had something else in store for him?

The man in question was into his fourth Ranji season, playing for Bihar. People knew him as a batsman who clobbered new-ball bowlers. But he hadn't done all that well in the past few seasons, and his journey up the ladder was rather stop-start. The East Zone representative in the national selection committee was more concerned about a wicketkeeper from the powerful state of Bengal.

Spotters Find Talent

But the then 22-year-old Mahendra Singh Dhoni carried on, multitasking with ease. It so happened that the BCCI sent two 'talent-spotters' of the Talent Resource Development Wing, instructing them to hop from one match to another. It was during one such game that Raju Mukherjee, the former Bengal skipper, noticed Dhoni. He was astonished to watch this lad hitting with tremendous power. Mukherjee's colleague, Prakash Chandra Podar, who played for Bengal in the 1960s, also witnessed Dhoni's prowess.

A casual exchange of notes between these talent spotters meant Dhoni had made the 'Talent Spotted' list. Consequently, his name found a place on the website of the National Cricket Academy. It was the first week of January 2004. The report went to Dilip Vengsarkar, the chairman of the wing. A superb talent spotter himself, Vengsarkar got cracking. He wanted the others to watch Dhoni and that included Kiran More, the chief selector at the time.

Dhoni and a few other talented boys were asked to report to the NCA. He knew right away that he was on the selectors' radar and he did what he knew best – attack bowlers. But behind the stumps, he was clumsy. So much so that someone sarcastically remarked, "No wonder he was the goalkeeper of the school's football team."

Within six months, Dhoni, the 'clobber man' of Ranchi was in the India 'A' team touring Kenya. Ranchi erupted in joy. Little did they know that Dhoni would give them many more reasons to celebrate.

Ranchi didn't exactly have a cricketing culture. In Jamshedpur, which is a four-hour drive from Ranchi, the House of Tatas patronized cricket. There was a time when Bihar had Ramesh Saxena, a stylish batsman who toured England with the Indian team in 1967. They also had Daljeet Singh, who missed out on the 1970 tour of the West Indies, leg-spinner Anand Shukla and Hari Gidwani, an elegant stroke player. These players, who had migrated from Delhi, were recruited by TISCO chairman Russi Mody, an ardent sports lover.

Dhoni's selection surprised the cricket lovers of Kolkata because the other candidate, Deep Dasgupta, was already a Test player. How could the two talent spotters, both former Bengal players, mind you, pick someone else? On the tour of Kenya, Dhoni's exploits with the bat led to his promotion in the batting order. His strike-rate was phenomenal. Coach Sandeep Patil, an attacking batsman himself, approved of Dhoni's dare-devilry.

While the support staff and captain kept pushing him higher up the order, Dhoni remained the same batsman – No. 7 or No. 3, he never altered his style or approach. Mumbai's Ramesh Powar was also on that tour. "We all knew each other well but nobody, not even the player from Bengal, knew Dhoni. He was quiet and shy. He would occupy the rear seat on the team bus. In one match against Pakistan 'A', the two of us had a big partnership. He hardly spoke after the over and he continues to be the same. Frankly speaking, standing at the non-striker's end, I was scared because the ball would fly off his bat like a rocket. On one occasion, when a Pakistani bowler asked the umpire to stand a bit closer to the stumps, the umpire retorted loudly, "Do you want me to die?"

Within three months, Dhoni was in the Indian team for the tour of Bangladesh. What happened there would have put the best of fantasy writers to shame. Dhoni did not leave any room for interference. He wasn't at the mercy of the selectors. He constantly scored and scored big. He grabbed every chance, consistently churning out 'impact' knocks.

The TRDW helped Dhoni's fate by spotting and fast tracking him, but it was the Kiran More-led selection committee which gave him the opportunity. In a team game like cricket, where one slot could open up a world of opportunities, giving someone that 'golden chance' can make a lot of difference. Says More, "The first time I watched him was in the Ranji one-dayers. He was a hard hitter. The best part was that he wasn't a slogger. He was middling the ball very well. We were looking for a wicketkeeper-batsman for the Indian team as Rahul Dravid was being over-burdened. I met Dhoni in Bangalore and gave him some tips about wicket keeping. He was quick to make those adjustments. Greg Chappell, too, was impressed with his batting."

Talent spotting is an art. Kudos to the two gentlemen who did their job seriously! Also, let's give Vengsarkar and More credit for fast-tracking Dhoni into the Indian team. Every cricketer needn't go through the grind. Some are just born to play at the biggest stage. Dhoni is certainly one of them.

Chappell agrees with More. "The first time that I sat up and took notice of MS Dhoni was during a training camp at the M Chinnaswamy Stadium in Bangalore in mid-2005. He was batting in the nets at the BEML end of the ground with Ajit Agarkar amongst the bowlers. On what was a slow, low practice pitch, Dhoni looked quite comfortable on the front foot so I asked Ajit to test him with a bouncer. Ajit had a very good bouncer that often surprised batsmen, especially on slower wickets.

He bowled a beauty – not too short, rising to about

Adam's apple height over the right shoulder. Dhoni, unfazed, rocked back onto his back foot and hit the ball as hard and high, in front of square, as I had ever seen a ball struck. The ball rocketed up to hit the fascia of the stand above the playing field. The sound of ball hitting bat, and ball hitting fascia, seemed to be simultaneous. It was one of the most audacious shots I had ever seen. Had it not hit the fascia of the stand, it would have landed in the Police Parade Ground, hundreds of metres away, on Link Road!

"During that same camp, we had some sessions of simulated match practice aimed at improving the team's ability to chase targets in one-day matches. The recent history in run chases was extremely poor. It soon became apparent that Dhoni was one of the best 'finishers' in this format.

"With Dhoni in this role, India has become one of the best chasers in world cricket. He can hit a six on any ground in the world and he can do it on demand. Dhoni's grounding in tennis-ball cricket is obvious in the way he bats. He has an inimitable and unorthodox technique. With his strength, he is capable of hitting balls into places, few others can conceive. He is the best attacking player of the Yorker I have ever seen. I once saw him hit a James Anderson Yorker straight back over the Englishman's head for a six. It was awesome.

"The other thing that I soon learnt about Dhoni was that he really understood the game, that he had a calm confidence about his own ability and that he was not bothered with false modesty. If he thought he could do something, he was not scared to say so. Not in an egotistical

way, just forthright. This was also unique to Dhoni and I found it refreshing. Whenever I thought of Dhoni, I was reminded of the quote from Bhagavad Gita, "It is better to live your own destiny imperfectly than to live an imitation of someone else's life with perfection."

Dhoni's relationship with Chappell was a healthy one. To elicit such a response from a champion batsman, perhaps the best post-war exponent Australia has produced, is just awesome. And mind you, Chappell is not easy to impress. But in his own charming way, Dhoni came across as someone who meant business.

Soon, Dhoni became the darling of the masses, making himself indispensable even by staying in the background.

Brash, Brilliant

This was also a time when cricket saw the rise of another promising star. Unlike the more silent star Dhoni, Virat Kohli arrived loud and roaring. Leading his side to glory in the 2008 ICC Under-19 World Cup in Malaysia, Kohli looked brash. But his growth was rapid.

Off the field, the 23-year-old has been rather notorious, his actions often unleashing the 'child' in him. But on the field, he is a different person. Ever since his maiden first-class season in 2006-07, he has steadily grown into a complete player with his mature performances.

He has constantly churned out match-winning knocks. In the 2012 Adelaide Test against Australia, he became the only Indian to score a century on that tour.

In the Commonwealth Bank tri-series that followed, his unbeaten 133, off just 86 balls, against Sri Lanka in Hobart was phenomenal. Less than two weeks later, he smashed his way to a sensational 183 against Pakistan in Dhaka at the Asia Cup.

Watching Kohli tackle the Australian bowlers Down Under was like a breath of fresh air. And his 183 against arch-rivals Pakistan prompted former India skipper and spin legend Bishan Singh Bedi to call up his coach. All Bedi wanted was Kohli's number. Bedi didn't get through to Indian cricket's present day superstar, but the lad was gracious enough to return the call.

Says Bedi, "I told him I would love to shake hands. He's a tremendous talent but my only worry is he shouldn't go berserk. I feel he needs to work on his temperament a bit. All that aggression and jumping around doesn't go down well on these shores."

Kohli is perceived as the magic boy of Indian cricket. And like Bedi, there are others who are concerned about his 'handling'. Kohli is to be handled with care, lest the magic vanishes. Sachin Tendulkar aired similar views on his return from Dhaka. "He is a very good player, he is brilliant. He has done very well. But all I can say is don't put pressure on him. Let him enjoy his game."

At the same time, the magical fingers did not emerge overnight. True, the purple patch he is going through is unprecedented. But people – peers, coaches, selectors, senior players and teammates – who've watched him from his junior days always knew he was meant for greater things. Kohli had displayed enormous talent and commendable temperament very early in life. Combined with an intelligent brain, he becomes a prized repository for the future.

After tasting success at the Under-19 World Cup, Kohli was awarded the India cap the same year, in August 2008, against Australia. That was just two years after his first-class debut as an 18-year-old.

Not many know what happened during the course of Kohli's first-class debut. In many ways, it made him the person he is, strong and determined. Little did he know that his debut season, match rather, would define the rest of his life. The teenager was forced to grow up into a responsible man sooner than he'd have wanted.

Delhi was hosting Karnataka at the Ferozeshah Kotla on December 19, 2006. Kohli's team was staring at a follow-on. What's more, Delhi was facing the threat of relegation to the Plate Group in the Ranji Trophy. The mood in the dressing room was sombre. Kohli's father, Prem, had passed away that very morning. A sobbing Kohli quietly informed his coach and the two arrived at a consensus that he would continue to bat.

The way Kohli played that day remains etched in the memory of skipper Mithun Manhas and all the others who watched him. Batting along with Puneet Bisht who scored a 156-run knock, Kohli helped Delhi avoid the follow-on by scoring 90 runs. "He had a blank expression on his face but was determined from within. It was he who did the talking in the middle. He kept telling me to concentrate and play straight."

At the close of play, Delhi had saved the match and Kohli

went home to attend his father's cremation. His immense personal loss was laced with tears of anguish as he felt that the umpire had made the wrong decision. Later that day, he called Bisht to congratulate him on his performance.

If this isn't character, what is? Every time he faced a ball during that innings, his childhood days may have flashed past. To lose a loved one is painful enough; to do your job in the face of such adversity is something altogether different. And that's something lesser mortals can't even imagine.

Kohli's journey from a Delhi lad to India's batting sensation had no shortcuts. He wasn't from the league of players who took the IPL route to Team India. He has risen through the ranks playing age-group cricket and two seasons of solid first-class cricket. He was barely 14 when he played his first league match in Delhi's 'A' division. He hit a 251 against Himachal Pradesh then and has two double centuries in both Under-15 and Under-17 cricket.

As a middle-order batsman, Kohli is solid in defence and can play all around the wicket. But he is particularly lethal on the leg side. He has an array of strokes – he plays the pull shot as authoritatively as anyone – and has shown that he can play the short-pitched delivery very well by taking it on his body and keeping it down.

Three years after his ODI debut, Kohli got the coveted Test cap during the tour of the West Indies in Kingston in June 2011. Till date, he has played 24 Tests and has scored 1721 runs with an average of 46.51 and hit 6 hundreds. His ODI career, which started in August 2008 against Sri Lanka in Dambulla, is 134 matches old and he already has

19 centuries and 30 half centuries to his credit. His average in blue clothing is a phenomenal 52.16.

Right Man for the Big Job

As the youngest Delhi batsman in Team India, his stint as vice-captain (in the 2012 Asia Cup) started with a furious round of speculation. People were already calling him Dhoni's successor in all formats. With Virender Sehwag opting for rest and Gautam Gambhir being bypassed, a significant message was being sent by the national selectors. Kohli was being earmarked as the future captain of India. The selectors have reportedly had a word with Dhoni regarding his future plans.

Rumours were abound that Dhoni had informed the selectors about his desire to prolong his ODI and Twenty20 careers. And he wants them to start nurturing his successor for the Test role. If this is indeed the case, Kohli can be groomed. "I think that is a very good idea. We will be investing in the future," says Bedi.

Detractors quote Kohli's youthfulness as a drawback. However, it must be remembered that young he may be, but responsibility is not new to Kohli. Having led Delhi ably, he has all the qualities for the big job. In fact, a young Kohli is known to have made field changes in domestic matches, leaving his skipper surprised! He even ticked off two senior players in the Delhi side, asking them to be serious on the field!

When Aakash Chopra, the captain of Delhi, got injured

in the 2009-10 season, Kohli performed the rescue act in two matches. In fact, it so turned out that the matches which Kohli led were the only ones Delhi won that season. Kohli led from the front, coming out to open the batting in the second innings in one of the matches.

Kohli is the gem India were looking for. While he should be handled with care and used with caution, another aspect that worries the experts is his temper. Naturally aggressive, his 'angry young man' and 'brash' image is a cause for concern.

Hari Gidwani, a former Delhi player and selector, has a critical analysis to offer. "When I first watched Virat after the Under-19 World Cup victory, I could not accept his behaviour. I personally thought it was not good for an upcoming youngster to display so much aggression and arrogance on the field."

From the year 2008 to 2011, I served Delhi as a Ranji selector and had a good look at this boy. He looked very promising and technically very sound. His batting was all about timing. He bats the same way in the IPL, too, and even his lofted shots are well-timed. The only thing I used to fear was his penchant for playing across the line. Funnily enough, he'd always get a boundary. This shot may not help him on seaming and bouncy wickets, though.

As Gidwani continues, "Once, at the Roshanara ground during a Ranji Super League game, I was disappointed with his performance. He was getting a tad impatient and playing rash strokes in a difficult situation. I screamed from the sightscreen area, asking him to relax. He immediately told me to mind my own business. I was a little hurt. After all, everyone was watching. Many journalists asked me, but I ignored the comment. However, we met after the close of play and he said hello to me. However, he's a different man these days. I see him as a future India skipper. He is still not mature enough to lead the country right away. He has also realized that he is being groomed for the big role and that's brought about a change in his attitude these days."

There are many who will swear by what Gidwani has to say. Brijesh Patel, who works with the Royal Challengers Bangalore, has something different to share. "Initially, Virat was very aggressive at the crease. His shot selection was faulty. His technique wasn't sound but over the years, experience has taught him to think of his batting. He used to play across the line. He wasn't confident against the short stuff but he worked on his weakness. And now that he knows he is being groomed for the big job, he has calmed down. He thinks first, then acts. He definitely has leadership qualities."

Born Leader

Talk about leadership and you've got to take Dhoni's name. He has taken the entire cricketing world by storm. With unbelievable decisions, he is blessed with what he calls good cricketing sense. But Dhoni's captaincy is no less than a phenomenon. There has been no other leader to have evoked such awe.

Dhoni's ability to finish games seems like a part of his job profile. He does not bat like just another batsman; he bats like a captain. To say that he leads from the front is an understatement. He lets his boys do the job themselves and lest they falter, he comes towards the end and saves them all. If one looks at it, Dhoni's captaincy is based on the simple principle that one has to be calm and live in the present to deal with the situation. Be it his batting or his captaincy, Dhoni's mental strength is very much on view.

Dr Rudi Webster, who was the manager of the star-studded West Indies team and later at the Kerry Packer circus in 70s, has written a book titled *Think Like A Champion*, where he interviewed many psychological champions in cricket. Talking to him, Dhoni candidly says, "I see pressure as an opportunity to do well. If you are under pressure, you should not see it as a danger and give in to it. People say a lot of negative things about pressure. Pressure to me is just an added responsibility. That is how I look at it. It's not pressure when God gives you an opportunity to be a hero for your team and country. If you expect pressure and have a plan to deal with it, you will know exactly what to do when it comes, and more often than not, you will use it in a positive and productive way. The best way to deal with it is to stay in the moment and not get trapped in the past or caught up in the future of the result or on what might happen. If you stay in the moment, calm your mind and focus on the process you won't feel much pressure."

The Spirit to Succeed in the Face of All Odds

Easier said than done, one would say. But what distinguishes players like Virat Kohli and MS Dhoni from the others is that they have actually walked the talk. In the crunchiest of situations, they have delivered performances of substance. Pressure? What's that!

To get Dhoni to lose his temper is more difficult than taming a wild elephant; in Kohli's case, it is child's play. But different as these two players are, their hunger for success is quite similar. So is their fighting spirit. What Indian cricket needs is this continual belief that they can win and win anything.

Sourav Ganguly

Yuvraj Singh

What's the co-relation between left-handers and artistry? Why are they a connoisseur's delight? Be it cricket, tennis or even football, men who conjure up an image of creativity with their left hand or feet, are always adored. Sometimes revered, even worshipped.

Ever wondered why? Some things, they say, are better left unexplained. It shouldn't stop you from loving them, though.

They are your darlings. When they ply their trade, sport seems an art. Everything about them catches the eye – grace, style, flourish, even the walk. In cricket, hearts have been known to melt the moment a left-hander's bat meets the ball. But how a mere change of arms results in such difference, one might ask.

That's the moot point: it isn't just a shift from right to left; it's a change of perspective. Left-handers are to cricket what an oasis is to the Sahara: a whiff of fresh air, a welcome change. Southpaws – that's a term borrowed from boxing – provide an alternate side of cricket and a fresher one at that.

When a century ago, the tall and handsome Frank Woolley of England batted, cricket lovers would watch with twinkling eyes. It was said that no bowler felt humiliated with his stroke play because of the poise with which the ball was caressed to the boundary. Helpless bowlers could but smile in appreciation. The crowd had to gather their voices back from their gaping eyes to applaud. They had forgotten everything else but to see, to watch, Woolley bat. Woolley's sublime batting brought life into the stadium.

Sir Neville Cardus wrote about Woolley's batting in Cardus on Cricket: "His batsmanship, like all fine art, can be enjoyed by everybody, because it is fresh and natural, and, at bottom, as simple as it is modest. An innings by Woolley begins from the raw material of cricket and goes far beyond. Some of Woolley's innings stay with us until they become like poetry which can be told over again and again; we see the shapeliness of his cricket with our minds and we feel its beauty with our hearts."

The Prince of Calcutta

Reading these lines, poetry as it feels like itself, brings to mind a person much closer home. If he played in Cardus's times, these lines could have been very well written for Sourav Chandidas Ganguly. 'The Prince of Calcutta' is how Geoff Boycott rechristened Ganguly as. Ganguly's off-side shots won Boycott's heart, and he couldn't stop praising Ganguly on air. When Ganguly arrived on the international scene, his batsmanship was uncomplicated. With his head still and feet movements precise, he would meet the ball at a point which would make it go in the direction he desired. Woolley was revered for much the same skill.

At the crease, Ganguly was all grace. It didn't matter whether the fixture was a Test match or a One-Day International. He was a master at assessing the situation, a lord at pacing the innings and a thorough professional who played for the team. While it's common knowledge that he was at his attacking best in limited-overs cricket, the innings of his that readily comes to mind was that hundred on Test debut. At Lord's, the spiritual home of cricket and the most hallowed of grounds, Ganguly's strokes were compared to the ones that came off the willow of David Gower, the golden boy of English cricket in the 1980s.

'Chocolate Boy', Tough Lad

If Ganguly used his bat as a spatula while driving square of the wicket, then Yuvraj Singh presented a completely different picture. Another leftie-par-excellence, the Chandigarh lad was called 'chocolate boy'. There was nothing chocolaty about his batting, though.

The elegance of a left hander does surface in his shot selection, but unlike Ganguly, Yuvraj's style is meant to destroy the opposition. When in the mood, and form, he can match every Sir Garfield Sobers shot for shot – front- and back-foot drives on both the flanks, cuts and flicks with tremendous power, pulls, hooks et al. His well-timed shots give the fielders no time to react.

His father, Yograj Singh, built a gymnasium on the first floor of their Sector 11B house and bought a dozen bats, and a bagful of cricket and tennis balls. The Shivalik Hills, with all its scenic beauty, stood behind their blooming garden. But Yograj wasn't bothered about beauty; his concern was stamina. He uprooted the garden – yes, literally – and prepared a small pitch where he and Yuvi began practising from dawn to dusk, and beyond. Academics, like everything else, became secondary.

It's My (Dad's) Life!

As a kid, Yuvi loved skating. He'd won a sub-junior championship in school but Yog wouldn't have any of it. Instead of giving the boy a pat on the back, he threw away the skates and ordered Yuvi never to skate competitively again. Yuvi's competitiveness, his father thought, had to be preserved for cricket. Yuvi had to become a cricketer. Not a skater, not anything else. His fate was sealed and no one could challenge it. The very purpose of his birth was to complete the prophecy of Yograj's ambition.

Rise, Shine and Pain

Yog would drag Yuvi out of bed as early as 4 am in the peak of winter. I was at their Chandigarh home when I heard Yuvi scream. Concerned, I went to the place where they were practicing only to see him rub his chest, which had been badly hit by a hard wet tennis ball. The tender pink-chested boy, all of 12, was in pain. The point of impact had turned black and blue. All Yuvi could do was wait for the pain to lessen and then get back to practice. I tried to convince Yog that 12 hours of practice would kill the boy's love for the game. But Yog being Yog wanted his son to learn things the hard way. Some parents are like that. They are taskmasters. But you can never doubt their intentions. They only want their kids to be the best. Yuvi may or may not have understood his father completely.

Says Bishan Singh Bedi, "Even at the Under-14 level,

Yuvi was unusually big for his age. He was tremendously talented and hit the cricket ball with enormous power. In our summer camps in Chail (Himachal Pradesh), which is the highest cricket ground in the world, we'd lose many balls thanks to Yuvi's big hitting. While lads of his age group would struggle to reach the ropes, Yuvi would clear them with ease. He hit the ball so long (and so often) that it could not be retrieved from down the hill."

Bedi had to find a solution to this interesting but unusual problem? "To stop his big hitting, we made a rule. When the ball went over the hill, Yuvi would be declared out!"

Bedi, a former India skipper and one of the best spinners the world has ever seen, vividly recalls Yuvraj's energy and mischief (the latter often bordered on indiscipline). "There were times when I'd drive him down the hill six or seven kilometres and then tell him to get off and jog behind my vehicle all the way up!" Bedi says.

Balvinder Singh Sandhu, the former India medium pacer who played a stellar role in the final of the 1983 World Cup, met Yuvi when he was an innocent 16-year-old. "Yuvi was extremely talented, but he loved to loft the ball. He was confused because his coaches had told him not to loft. Perhaps they were right because he sometimes lofted without employing the proper technique and often ended up getting caught in the deep," Sandhu recalls of their meeting at a camp organized by the Punjab Cricket Association in 1997.

Talent, they say, is as good as zilch if not backed by technique and, of course, temperament. All Sandhu did was nurture Yuvi's talent and give it direction. "I showed him the technique to loft, and I saw to it that he sincerely practised it," he says. On his day, Yuvraj's glorious lofts can make the Dale Steyns and Brett Lees look like maidan bowlers.

Yuvraj's first love, however, remained tennis. He often felt the pressure of cricket being a team sport. After being dropped after his debut Ranji Trophy game against Orissa, his resentment towards team sports grew. For the next two years, he could only play junior matches.

Play to Win

Meanwhile, Yuvi's father kept the pressure on, making sure his son persevered. The tour of England, with Kailash Gattani's team, changed Yuvi's outlook a great deal. He ended up topping the batting charts and his game seemed visibly tight, but most importantly, I could see he had finally realized the values of the game.

Gattani recounts the endeavours of a 16-year-old Yuvraj. "He came with me on the tour of England in 1997. And he was a big hit. He was a brilliant batsman with loads of guts. In one of the matches, we were faced with a very difficult call, one that every Test team faces. We could either draw the game or risk it and go for the win. To me, and others in the team, a draw seemed the most practical option. But Yuvi was way too confident. He wanted to win. He batted like a king and we won the game with a few overs to spare. The fielding side protected the long-on and long-off boundaries, but like a warrior up for the challenge, Yuvi kept hitting those huge sixes." This time, no one declared him out!

In fact, Yuvraj made his Test debut in 2003 after Ganguly was laid low by injury. But once Ganguly returned, Yuvi was dropped. The following year, he got his second opportunity when – who else – Ganguly was rendered unavailable for the Pakistan tour.

A smart cricketer is an opportunist, so to speak. And Yuvi made it count, and how. He scored a century in the second Test at Lahore. India lost that match, and when Ganguly returned for the third Test, the selectors put their faith in Yuvi. It was Aakash Chopra who had to sit out.

Initially, Yuvi got the chance to display his amazing batting skills only when Ganguly was unavailable. But as Yuvi slowly but steadily cemented his place in the national side, it was the same Ganguly who played an important role – that of moulding Yuvraj.

Every sportsperson yearns for a mentor, a guide. In the unforgiving world of an Indian cricketer, replete with one flight after another, press conferences, autographs, photographs, promotional events, cameras, flashlights and, of course, cricket, a player could lose his sanity. What you need at that point in time is someone to shield you, support you. Your parents, friends and well-wishers would certainly offer help, but it wouldn't make much of a difference. The only persons who can help you 'handle' this fame and the pressures that go with it are those who've 'been there, done that'.

And just like that, Yuvi found a mentor in Ganguly. He worshipped him. I clearly remember our conversations with Yuvi, and how much he respected 'Dada'.

In Yuvi, Ganguly saw an opener of the calibre of Sehwag. But the move failed. A few poor outings in the Border-Gavaskar Trophy against Australia and Yuvraj was dropped in favour of Gautam Gambhir.

In 2005, Sachin Tendulkar's tennis elbow paved the way for Yuvraj's re-entry. But what cemented Yuvraj's place in the team was his dear captain's downfall. Greg Chappell took to these shores like a storm and swept away the man who was the face of the revolutionary change in Indian cricket.

The Chappell Era

Ganguly was sacked ruthlessly. Yes, the man who taught India and its fans to win was gone. Just like that. The historic 2-1 series win over Steve Waugh's 'Invincibles' was conveniently forgotten. So was the unbelievable victory in the 2002 NatWest Trophy in England. Why, even the manner in which he led an inspired and talented but underrated bunch to the final of the 2003 ICC World Cup was overlooked.

Captain Ganguly fell and the nation gulped in shock. Yuvraj loved his captain dearly. With his departure, Ganguly also passed on the title of 'Prince' to his understudy. A disappointed but determined Yuvraj accepted it gracefully.

In cricket, timing is paramount. You may have built an empire, brick by brick, but that doesn't mean you occupy the seat of power forever. Why do you think we have words and phrases like 'successors', 'planning for the future', 'passing the torch', etc. Everyone loves to stay. The key is to know when to leave. You've got to get the timing right. And this rule applies to everyone. Take a leaf out of Ratan Tata's book and you'll know what I'm trying to say.

Yuvraj scored a century, his second in Test cricket, in the third Test against Pakistan in 2006. And again, India lost. Yuvraj struggled as the season progressed and also got injured. Call it fate, destiny or whatever you want, but Yuvraj's injury meant Ganguly was back in the side. Buoyed by his stellar domestic performances, Dada subsequently top-scored in his return series and sealed his place.

Ganguly and Yuvraj, two stylish, assertive left-handers who respected each other, were in a strange mesh. One's inclusion meant the sacking of the other. Numerous rounds of kho-kho later, Yuvraj made his way back into the side when Tendulkar was out with injury. India were 61/4 before Yuvi and Ganguly stitched a 300-run partnership, with Yuvraj recording his highest Test score of 169. However, what followed was another poor run again against the Aussies, and he was dropped again.

Over the years, Yuvraj had earned a lot of experience in the middle order, but he could never cement his place in the Test side. He had to wait for someone to get injured to get a look-in. This is, no doubt, frustrating. But let's look at the bright side of things. There have been many great batsmen in India who simply could not get to wear a Test cap because of a packed middle order. Yuvraj, at least, got his chances.

Dilip Vengsarkar was the chairman of the national selection committee then. "Any type of injury annoys a player, especially when you have to sit out of Test matches. Yuvi suffered a knee injury while playing kho-kho, a traditional sport supposed to be played barefoot. He played with his shoes on, and paid a heavy penalty. When there is competition in the team, one has to be careful. It's not the player's fault every time, but once you've injured your knees or back, you are all the more conscious. You are not the same player after these injuries," Vengsarkar explains.

It took Yuvi six weeks of treatment and rest to recover from the injury – officially, that is – but the tale of his woes was much longer, almost never-ending. Imagine Superman with restricted flying powers. Yuvi's swift movements had deserted him. He tried to salvage the situation by ceasing to attempt those flamboyant dives on the field. Risk-aversion is sometimes necessary. But then again, there's no glory without guts. Yuvi channelled his energies to his batting instead. From a swashbuckler, he turned into a batsman who started playing calculated, percentage shots.

While Yuvi's career graph went up and down like a wave, Ganguly's life was characterized with very clear highs and lows. It was Ganguly who strongly recommended that Chappell be made head coach after John Wright's departure. What followed was a whirlpool of controversy. Never before had Indian cricket witnessed a captain-coach feud so intense, so ugly and so destructive. Both individuals were expressive and were legends in their own right. Alas, neither was ready to bow down. They had agreed to disagree on every issue on and off the field. It didn't matter if the issue was contentious or trivial.

Ganguly, the Phenomenon

If one thinks dispassionately, Ganguly was the best thing to have happened to Indian cricket. The game was in a mess after the match-fixing saga in 2000. Taking over as captain in normal circumstances is one thing; handling a demoralized, disillusioned bunch is another. Ganguly, with all his charisma and tenacity, proved he was a born leader. A fantastic manager of men indeed.

If Tiger Pataudi brought about a sense of responsibility among his players and got rid of that 'complex' so deeply rooted in their psyche, then Ganguly made his players realize that they had the potential to steamroll any team in the world.

Ganguly's real test came against world champions Australia, the pre-eminent team of our times, led by the great Steve Waugh. The Australians were on a mission: they wanted to crush India in India. They'd even given their mission a fancy name: The Final Frontier.

Ganguly adopted, rather embraced, Waugh's very own process of 'mental disintegration'. And he caught them unawares. Ganguly didn't mind defying tradition. His (supposedly intentional) late arrival for the toss put off the Australians much before the match began. And when the

Australian media criticized him, he didn't react. That made them angrier!

With Waugh's theory of 'mental disintegration' dealt with and binned, the Indians attacked from ball one. The nation was ecstatic. India had found a leader, a true one at that.

Ganguly was the last man who would cling on to sentiments while choosing his playing XI. He was always on the hunt for an effective combination. And this is how he discovered an opener in Sehwag. His move surprised everyone. It was criticized because Sehwag was everything but an opener. In fact, he was a perfect slogger and could flay attacks batting lower down the order.

It was reported that most of the selectors, and players, were against this notion. To them, exposing Sehwag to the new ball was a bit like investing in a sick industrial unit. Ganguly had no such concerns, though. He had immense faith in Sehwag. Perhaps, it had a lot to do with the Delhi batsman's hand-eye coordination and, of course, temperament. And Ganguly wanted this faith to resonate through the opposition ranks. Sehwag reflected the brave new face of India. He was ready to attack. He believed the only way to beat the opposition was to take the 'attack' route.

With Sehwag at the top, he was looking for a quick 100 on the board. That done, he had Rahul Dravid, Sachin Tendulkar, VVS Laxman and himself to take it from there. As an opener, Sehwag proved to be a phenomenon and, in many ways, was majorly responsible for changing the approach of Indian cricket.

Ganguly tried something similar with Yuvraj in 2004. He pushed him to open. This time, the move didn't click. With all his genius, Ganguly wasn't flawless. No captain succeeds all the time. Even the great Richie Benaud didn't. Nor did Ian Chappell. A good captain is one who makes things happen and Ganguly did just that.

Ganguly was a thinking captain, a visionary. To him, his players were his 'boys'. And he kept them together. Picture this: he was more like a superb HR manager – trying to identify the various skill sets at his disposal and assigning tasks accordingly. More often than not, he challenged his resources. Someone who was good just at one particular job/function was asked to acquire another skill, and eventually perfect it. He was a team builder. A bloody good one.

The End Game

But the game of thrones is a cruel one. You don't occupy the seat of power forever. Ganguly was sacked, and then dropped. Did he remain the same player after losing his place in the team? Definitely not. The selectors were weary of him. The media was having one field day after another. Ganguly was desperate to make a comeback, but Kiran More was unwilling to take the risk. Eventually, when Vengsarkar became the chairman of selectors, Ganguly was brought back. But the spark that was so characteristic of Ganguly was missing. He still managed to push and prod and made some good scores batting at No. 6. It was a position he enjoyed batting at. For, it allowed him to attack at will. He knew that that his position was safe as long as he scored runs. But it didn't help. Soon, he found himself out of the team, having been dropped unceremoniously.

This is what Chappell has to say about Ganguly in retrospect. "Sourav was an extremely good player for much of his career. His strength when he came in to international cricket was on the off side, so when teams began to give him less room he did not adapt well enough and develop his leg side game."

It may be recalled that Ganguly had sought help from Chappell ahead of the 2003-04 tour of Australia. "When he came to Sydney to work with me, I believe I was able to help him to play on the leg side as well as the off side. We worked on him not committing to the front foot too early so that he was able to go to where the ball was pitched rather than commit straight forward early and have to play around his front leg which had caused him some problems previously. Sourav worked hard and by the end of the week was getting in to much better positions," Chappell added.

"He went back to India and continued to work on what we had discussed. He scored a century soon after and then came to Australia in good form. His innings of 144 in the first Test in Brisbane was an outstanding innings that contributed largely to India drawing the Test on a very seam-friendly pitch. He didn't quite reproduce that form again on the tour and then slipped back into his old habits. By the time I got to India (remember it was Ganguly who helped Chappell land the coach's job) he was struggling and was very focused on just holding onto his place in the team. I tried to impress upon him that he should consider giving up the captaincy to focus on resurrecting his batting career. He resisted and the rest, as they say, is history," Chappell further wrote.

"Interestingly, when he came back into the side, he actually played quite well for a period which only reinforces my belief that, had he been prepared to give up the captaincy, he could have played on successfully as a batsmen for a few more years."

Ganguly, of course, thought differently.

Was Ganguly guilty of delaying Yuvraj's entry into Test cricket? Yes. Whenever Yuvraj replaced an injured Ganguly, he displayed tons of class. That brilliant hundred in Pakistan prompted the legends there – the likes of Hanif Mohammad, who'd played between 1952 and 1969, compare him to none other than Sobers. At No. 6, his job was to attack bowlers who were into their third spell, most often with the second new ball.

Yuvraj's knock against Pakistan in Bangalore again overshadowed Ganguly's batting. But quite shockingly, Yuvraj had to make way for Ganguly. And remember Yuvraj, unlike Ganguly, has always been a brilliant fielder. As a fielder, Ganguly was, at best, reluctant.

Breaks are of supreme significance in the life of a professional cricketer. Yuvraj was on an unending break, receiving an occasional invite to a game of musical chairs. He was never allowed to blossom.

If Ganguly was the Prince of Calcutta, Yuvraj was no less revered. His popularity soared to crazy heights after he

hammered Stuart Broad for six sixes in an over in a crunch game during the inaugural World Twenty20 in South Africa in 2007. He was well and truly the Sobers of India. The great man said, "I tend to agree".

To demolish international attacks at will, you need guts as much as you need skill. His power-packed shots had a slaughtering effect on the bowlers. The more they sledged him, the farther the subsequent delivery travelled.

Yuvi's World Cup

The 2011 World Cup changed everything in Yuvraj's life – his career, cricket, his very idea of life. His health was deteriorating by the day, and Yuvraj had no clue. Match after match, he carried a life-threatening tumor between his lungs. So what do you think kept him going?

In a way, sport is funny. You could shut yourself from the world, be oblivious to the hullabaloo around, and still inspire yourself to scale a peak. Yuvraj was chasing his dream. The India jersey brought the best in him. It also fetched him the 'Man of the World Cup' trophy. He was like God, more or less. What ensued brought even his detractors closer. The body had had enough. It cracked. Yuvi was diagnosed with cancer and it took him months to get life back on track.

After the huge controversy over his sacking, Ganguly made many a comeback into the Indian team. Watching him bat wasn't a pleasure all the time. It was miserable to see him struggle to make the XI.

Thanks, Dada

The 2008 home series against Australia would be his last and Ganguly went out on a high, scoring 324 runs in four Tests. The fourth Test in Nagpur was the last of his 113 appearances in white flannels. And like a chap called Bradman, he bowed out without troubling the scorers. Soon after he made that stunning "One last things, lads" announcement on the eve of the series opener in Bangalore, Dada had assured himself of a grand farewell. Four Tests, eight innings, countless standing ovations later, he was gone with his head held high.

India has always produced brilliant cricketers. But as a team, they were not what you would call winners. Often, they would crumble under pressure; occasionally, they would fall like a pack of cards. Not all of Ganguly's contributions can be quantified. He is more than just India's second most successful captain of all time (MS Dhoni holds that honor). A revolution is often sparked by an idea. Ganguly was that spark. And his 'play to win' ideology was the tonic Indian cricket needed. His approach mirrored the nation's sentiment. India was progressing and at some rate.

Alas, there was no place for Ganguly in his team. Yuvraj was a product of Ganguly's captaincy. Ganguly made Yuvraj what he is. And it was Yuvraj who took over, making people believe that Ganguly was no longer needed.

However, the most heartening and, perhaps, the most important fact is that Ganguly had failed to meet the standards he'd set for the rest. His team only cared about winning. In other words, there was no room for mediocrity. But even in his absence, it was always 'Ganguly's team'.

And it is through players like Yuvraj, Harbhajan Singh, Sehwag and Zaheer Khan that Ganguly lives on. Yuvraj's career, much like Ganguly's, has been a roller-coaster ride. What is also common is the impact they have made on Indian and world cricket. They are your larger-than-life personalities: they are either in or out, big or nothing. They are so honest, so alive, so emotional and so real.

Anil Kumble

Harbhajan Singh

Series after series, tournament after tournament, anybody and everybody frets over the composition of the Indian team. Do we have sound openers? Is the middle order potent enough? Will the tail stand up? So we need a third seamer? Are our pacers good enough to give us the early breakthrough? There is one area, however, that we seldom worry about. The spin department is India's own. This department has always delivered the goods. And it continues to shoulder the burden of wicket-taking.

Right from the time of Vinoo Mankad, Subhash Gupte and Ghulam Ahmed to the present lot of spinners, India has always produced world-class tweakers. And they have mesmerized year after year. In the 1970s, the Australians would sing "If Lillee doesn't get you, Thommo will." The crowd would get into the act and the so-called 'jingle' would demotivate the batsmen and rejuvenate Dennis Lillee and Jeff Thomson.

When the West Indies toured India in 1974-75, most batsmen struggled against the spinners. A West Indian journalist kept humming, "If Bedi can't get you, Chandra will." And with Prasanna making the batsmen dance to his tunes, India almost won the series. Eknath Solkar and S Abid Ali, the two specialist fielders in the 'leg trap', would be ready to pounce on any and every offering. At a private party, opener Roy Fredricks remarked, "Maaaan, as if facing those vicious spinning deliveries wasn't scary enough, there used to be that little Solkar intimidating the batsman from forward short-leg."

Your strength is often your opponent's weakness. And you never let go of that chance. Thanks to Tiger Pataudi, the Indians did just that. And yes, the spinners benefited the most.

Tricks of the Trade

Those were the days when pitches were uncovered. In India, spinners got into the act as early as the third over. Ali and Solkar would bowl the first two overs as 'formality'. In fact, Bedi would start loosening his joints as soon as he took to the field. But when covered pitches became the norm, India's strategy required modification. Over the first three days, the pitches were generally placid. The natural wear and tear aided spin on Days Four and Five. That India is the home of spin bowling can be said with authority and pride because the new batch of spinners have adjusted to the conditions and continued India's supremacy in this area. The challenges faced by the newer lot are far tougher than the ones their yesteryear counterparts were posed with.

India's love affair with spin continues. Anil Kumble and Harbhajan Singh have been among the greatest flag bearers of India's excellence in the spin department. Their place in the team was seldom under threat. Relentlessly complementing each other, they bowled thousands of overs together, winning many a match and series. Whatever the situation and whoever the captain, the duo was looked up to till Kumble retired in 2008.

Come to think of it, the bowler who went on to take 619 Test wickets – by far the most by an Indian bowler –

was criticized by one and all when he was picked for the England tour of 1990. Raj Singh Dungarpur, the chief selector, reacted by saying this was a team of the 90s.

Renowned former cricketers who had watched the Gupte brothers (Subhash and Baloo), VV Kumar and many others felt Kumble was too straight a spinner. He neither turned the ball nor spun it. He was a fastish bowler who, at best, was accurate. Once, in 1995, Dungarpur asked Bob Simpson, then a consultant to the Indian team, to help Kumble with his variations. Mind you, the 'exercise' was carried out at the Oval Maidan in full public view. No international player would have allowed this, but Kumble didn't mind. He was beyond petty ego issues.

Vinod Kambli was Kumble's contemporary. "We shared a room during the Irani Cup tie in 1990. Both of us were part of the Rest of India reserves. When I played him first in the nets, I thought he was a medium pacer. I was told he was selected as a leg-spinner. But instead of spinning the ball, he was bowling out-swingers! At times, he would bowl a bouncer. In the match against Delhi, he got all wickets from off bouncers. I've always loved to step out and loft spinners, but his pace never allowed it. As a roomie, he was very quiet. He would carry his engineering books and study every evening."

Word had spread that Kumble was a studious cricketer. But matches are played on the field, not in classrooms. To achieve success in international cricket, a spinner must spin the ball. He has to have variety. Kumble was accurate. But he rarely turned the ball even on rank turners! His style was different. He would test the patience of a batsman.

The advantage of being accurate was that a captain could afford to have a set of close-in fielders for him. He knew his limitations and more importantly, knew how to overcome them.

Mr Perfect

Says Greg Chappell, "Kumble was one of the most professional cricketers that I worked with. His preparation was always meticulous. He prepared and planned for his success. It did not come by accident. His two great strengths were competitiveness and intelligence. I remember noting that every time he came off the field after bowling, his first port of call was to the computer analyst to review his bowling.

"Despite his engineering background, I didn't see him as a technophobe, so I was interested to ask him what was it that he was looking for when he watched the replays. He said he would look at two things: pace and length. I don't remember the exact speed, but he knew that he bowled his best in India when his pace was around 85 kph. With experience, he learnt to be slower through the air in Australia. As for length, he judged where he was hitting the batsman on the pad and realized that the knee-roll was the ideal length. If he was hitting the batsman below the knee-roll, he was too full. If he was hitting them above the knee-roll, he was too short. This proved to me that he was using his intelligence wisely. By keeping everything simple, he was able to keep himself focused on the key issues."

Kumble was not laden with miraculous skill. He was just very smart in using what he had. Known for his intelligence, he had a method of approaching the crease. The most important aspect of bowling was perfection in line and length.

Chappell's observation can help young spinners emulate such tactics. "The other thing that Kumble spoke about during a team meeting was how he used the umpire as a guide in his run-up. As he reached the umpire, it was a reminder to put in the full effort from that point right through his delivery stride. He evidently adhered to this process and that's why he was so very successful. Considering that Anil was not a big spinner of the ball, his record is a testimony to his thoroughness, intelligence and relentless commitment to his process which obviously worked."

The Feisty Sardar

Kumble's long-time bowling partner couldn't have been more different. Hailing from Jalandhar in Punjab, Harbhajan's keenness to keep bowling at the nets has made him what he is. When, as a teenager he bowled to Mumbai batsmen back home, coach Balvinder Singh Sandhu was so impressed he wanted the off-spinner to play for Mumbai.

Kambli recollects, "The Mumbai team was in Jalandhar for the Wills Trophy. I saw this skinny 17-year-old boy bowling at the nets. He spun the ball and also gave it a lovely loop. Though he didn't trouble me, he was certainly impressive. In the evening, some of us including, coach Sandhu, felt we should ask him to play for Mumbai. Later, when he came into the Indian team, he was a different bowler. He had obviously had worked quite hard on his bowling."

Harbhajan was but an unknown name when he was included in the Indian team for the tour of New Zealand. Coach Aunshuman Gaekwad had to plead with the selectors to include 'Bhajji' in the squad. On his previous tours of New Zealand with Prasanna and Venkatraghavan, Gaekwad had noticed that the Kiwis were average players of off-spin.

Seen as a typical north Indian youngster by many, Bhajji, according to Gaekwad, did not have much of a cricketing culture. "He was raw, but willing to work hard. I remember having worked with him on that tour. We would interact before, during and after the match every day. And because I, too, started my career as an off-spinner, Bhajji's typical off-spinners action impressed me."

As different as chalk and cheese. While Kumble was willing to overcome his limitations by working smart, Bhajji seemed ready to sweat it out in order to achieve perfection. Gaekwad noticed Bhajji was a gifted bowler. Bhajji had long and strong fingers, a pre-requisite for turning the ball and extracting bounce. His wrist position gave him that loop. Gaekwad knew that the young sardar had a bright future. It was a matter of time, exposure and experience that he would become a star by himself, Gaekwad thought.

Bhajji was always ready and eager to work hard. He was also ready to try what was told to him by someone experienced.

"Off the field, Bhajji struggled with his English. His troubles would start as soon as he woke up. Calling for his morning cuppa was a pain. The great thing about Bhajji is that he laughs at himself. Today, he speaks like a professor of English!"

Gaekwad has also witnessed Kumble's success as a spinner. When he took over as coach, Kumble was already an experienced bowler. Gaekwad observed the meticulous and strategic methods of Kumble. In fact, Kumble had a plan for everything. Impressed as anyone would be, Gaekwad found a fierce competitor in Kumble.

Says Gaekwad, "Being an educated cricketer, Anil was an exception. His intelligence and thought process made him different. He was a champion. There is a saying that champions don't do different things; they do things differently. Anil was certainly above the rest. A perfectionist, he always worked on developing something new at the nets.

"Unlike Warne, Anil was not big turner of the ball. But he knew his limitations well. He came up with his own brand of variations. It is imperative that a cricketer evolves. There's no other way to survive, rather excel, in international cricket. The moment he felt he was no longer effective, he would come with something different."

When Anil Kumble arrived on the international circuit, he had a high jump at the delivery stride. This gave him extra bounce and zip. However, with age, that zip was lost.

"But Kumble being Kumble (read smart), it took him little time to realize this problem. And he quickly changed his bowling style. He decided to run in slowly, and also bowl slower through the air. This helped him extract a little more turn and loop. "This action was totally different from what he started with. His straighter ones and wrong 'uns were more effective now. This is because the batsman had to adjust to the variable line and length," says Gaekwad.

Kumble made sure he kept reinventing himself. He never stopped trying and always found a way to surprise the batsman. Just when it looked like Kumble would fade away, he bounced back stronger than ever. His 'Perfect 10' against Pakistan is the stuff of dreams. He was the one bowler who operated without a break on that fateful day. No wonder he looked drained at the tea break.

Gaekwad had a word with Azhar. He wanted Kumble to get some rest. India was sure they had ample time to win the Test match. However, to everyone's surprise, Kumble insisted on continuing. After tea, Kumble finished the job like a champion.

The Pakistanis are anything but novices when it comes to handling spin. And yet, Kumble destroyed them. According to Gaekwad, Kumble's endless variety of spin bowling baffled the visitors. "As for me, Anil was guided by his own intuitions and worked hard on them to achieve what he achieved ultimately."

Talk about the effectiveness of a bowler and who better than the wicketkeeper to judge this? For the record, Nayan Mongia kept for Kumble for a decade. If a batsman of the caliber of Kambli thinks Kumble was difficult to step out to, imagine the plight of the men who kept for his champion spinner. What Farokh Engineer was to BS Chandrasekhar,

Mongia was to Kumble. No bowler can take complete credit for his success. Alert and smart wicketkeepers build the pressure so required to unsettle a batsman. Not only do wicketkeepers have to be technically sound, but they must also have sharp reflexes.

Says Mongia, Kumble's long-time teammate "Anil and I made our debut when on the tour of the UK in 1990. He was a fastish bowler. Though he was a spinner, his attitude was like that of a fast bowler's. He wanted a wicket off every ball. That doesn't happen in international cricket. When we started off, the wickets used to be uncovered. And in India, we used to prepare turners so that we could win inside three days. He was dangerous and would often extract sharp bounce. On placid wickets, he would focus on accuracy."

To list out Anil's great performances is not an easy job. Two years after gobbling up the Pakistanis in 1999, he became the first Indian spinner to take 300 Test wickets. And he achieved this stupendous feat on his home ground in Bangalore. The following year, in 2002, he did the same in ODIs. At The Oval in August 2007, he overtook Glenn McGrath's mark of 563 Test wickets. A few months later, he broke the magical 600-wicket barrier to gain membership to an ultra-elite club comprising just two others – Shane Warne and Muttiah Muralitharan.

Mongia had to train hard to keep for Kumble. "I worked on my reflexes and they improved. I could then read Anil's body language, release, googly and top-spinner. Initially, he used to run in straight but later he changed to a zig-zag run-up. We would often sit and discuss cricket."

Mongia occupied pride of place on that historic day in New Delhi. Mongia did not keep much for Bhajji, but they shared an extremely crucial partnership in the epic 2001 series against Australia.

Says Mongia, "Harbhajan was 18 when he played a Test. He was what every off-spinner would want to be. He had a very good floater and imparted good spin on the ball. Later, he changed his action in order to develop the doosra. The action was questioned and he was under immense pressure."

Bhajji's problems were mostly psychological. He didn't have much self-belief. At the international level, sportsmen need to be in the best of health and spirits. During his early days in international cricket, Harbhajan was a confident young man. In fact, it bordered on over-confidence and skipper Ganguly would have to control him on the field. There were instances when coach John Wright would be calming Bhajji's nerves. Harbhajan continued to excel because of favourable support.

The story took an unexpected turn when Chappell took over. His maxim was similar to that of Tiger Pataudi's. He believed that if a player was good enough to play international cricket, then he should be able to sort out minor issues on his own.

Change? No, Thanks

Harbhajan had gotten too comfortable. He was used to the methods of the earlier regime. Chappell and he were not on the same wavelength. Chappell's aim was to take each player to the next level. He expected them to trust him, but Bhajji was content with what he was doing. This is where the trouble started. Resistance to change is understandable but, in this case, both had agreed to disagree. Harbhajan's performance obviously suffered.

Here's Chappell on Harbhajan. "All I am prepared to say about Harbhajan is that I think he suffered from a lack of self-belief. He had the ability to spin the ball more than Kumble, but did not have Kumble's belief. Nor did he have the commitment, patience and consistency needed to become a great bowler. Harbhajan appeared to have an ad hoc approach to preparation and liked to have conditions in his favour to perform. His record away from the subcontinent appears to reflect this. Even his record in ODIs in India reflects that he was not a match-winner on home soil. Had he had more belief in himself, I believe he could have been one of India's best-performed spin bowlers."

Chappell's views will find very few refuters. Harbhajan did not make optimum use of his talent. Chappell's arrival changed a lot of things. On the contrary, Kumble remained his intelligent self, knowing when and how to evolve. His discussions with Chappell were frank and based on rationale. And most importantly, he was performing.

Harbhajan was just the opposite. His obsession with the doosra cost him a genuine floater. Some of the people who played with Prasanna felt Harbhajan's floater was as good as the legend's. However, the invention of the doosra raised many an eyebrow. His action was no longer clean. And his effectiveness suffered due to his IPL commitments. He began to bowl faster and in the process, lost his form of yore.

The moot point of difference between Harbhajan and Kumble was the fear of failure. Kumble's arrival in international cricket itself was on the basis of criticism. A player who was called a straight spinner in 1990 was a world class bowler by 2007. And quite certainly, he is among the greatest spinners cricket has seen. There were no shortcuts, no miracles. Kumble worked his butt off. And yes, he never lost faith in his abilities. Also, he was (still is) a large-hearted man. At Antigua in 2002, he bowled with a fractured jaw.

And at The Oval in 2007, he surprised everyone by scoring his maiden Test century 17 years into international cricket. He was soft but effective, polite but firm. Kumble has always been a great ambassador of Indian cricket. His statesman-like handling of the hugely controversial Monkeygate saga earned him a lot of admirers. He had built a reputation over the years.

During his time as captain, Kumble preferred to stick to the basics. He was more of a 'no risk' customer. That was his approach to his bowling too. He rarely experimented. Instead, he chose to keep bowling to his strengths. As a captain, he didn't make things happen. Nor did he lose sleep over the strengths, weakness and plans of the opposition. He struck to his guns and expected his team not to deviate from his plans.

Harbhajan had all the qualities to become the spinner of spinners, but the fear of failure got to him. Was it because of early success? Or did it have to do with the high hopes we had in him? Truth is that the Harbhajan we know, no longer exists. Bhajji still has lot of cricket left in him, though. As Gaekwad says, "In a nutshell, you can't buy experience and there is no shortcut to experience apart from working hard. Bhajji is a young bowler with experience and the right amount of skill. All he needs to do is execute his plans."

They say spinners attain 'maturity' in their 30s. But in the case of Harbhajan Singh, this doesn't hold good. He was a devastating bowler right from his teens. He was blessed with all the traits of a champion off-spinner. He also had a very good floater. But in his quest to emulate Saqlain Mushtaq and his doosra, Bhajji lost out his originality. The Harbhajan we see today is not the Harbhajan who bamboozled the Aussies in 2001. He bowls flat and he bowls a restrictive line. He bowls to stop the flow of runs. Earlier, he used to entice the batsman and induce mistakes. Now he waits for the batsman to err.

His obsession with the doosra prompted many to question his action. And one must say he overused the so-called variation in ODI cricket. More than 60 per cent of his deliveries would go the other way. He became way too predictable. He had to compromise with his other – and more potent – variations. He chose to contain the batsman instead of going for the kill. And in the process, his beautiful off-breaks – the ones that spun and bounced viciously – vanished. At the Test level, he became more and more predictable, so much so that the left-handers, who once danced to his tunes, began treating him like a novice. There was a time when they would fail to read his deliveries. Nowadays, they happily go onto the back foot and cut him through the point region.

All said and done, Kumble and Harbhajan together have given India's bowling attacks that stability, we so badly missed for many years. Thanks to them, India enjoyed a second golden era after the years of the quartet. Together, Kumble and Harbhajan recreated that period. There was no escaping them.

But they did try a little too hard to prolong their Test careers? One may be forced to nod in affirmation. Towards the fag end of his days as a Test bowler, Kumble struggled a lot. His fastish deliveries were promptly put away. The accuracy was missing. Harbhajan viewed R Ashwin as his competitor. Ashwin, on the other hand, quietly went about his business and stayed focused on the job at hand. Harbhajan received a lot of support from Dhoni, but the skipper seemed to have had enough. In fact, he stopped backing Harbhajan. Being the wicketkeeper, Dhoni knows what his bowlers are doing. He is in perfect position to assess the strengths and weaknesses of his bowlers. He realized that Harbhajan was no longer the Harbhajan of yore. He promptly invested time, energy and most importantly, his faith in Ashwin.

Fast bowlers have come and gone. But India owes much of its success in the past 10 years to this duo. Test match after Test match, Kumble and Harbhajan bowled in tandem. Shrewdly, they probed the opposition. They say bowlers hunt in pairs. And when Kumble quit, Harbhajan lost that much-needed support and guidance. Suddenly, he was the leader of the spin department. Maybe he wasn't prepared for the big role. Some bowlers perform only when they combine with their trusted partner. But to be fair, Kumble and Harbhajan did what was expected of them. We'll always be proud of them.

Shikhar Dhawan

Rohit Sharma

Ravindra Jadeja

India's cricketing history is filled with stories about legends. Legends they are and legends they will be but like everything else they, too, have an expiry date. As the years go by, even the best of players seem like excess baggage.

But it is not easy to drop these players. And as a result, they keep their place in the side because of who they are and not what they've done in the recent past. To put it simply, they are too big to be dropped, too influential to be discarded. The selectors think twice before giving them marching orders. These 'seniors' are always allowed to be in their comfort zone. They would score some runs and then stand in the slips, a position ideal for much-needed 'rest'. When the Australians arrived on these shores in 1969, chief selector Vijay Merchant sacked Chandu Borde and Rusi Surti, who later played for Queensland as a professional. Merchant had had enough of such seniors.

Merchant's decision was met with obvious hue and cry. Borde had represented India for more than a decade and even though he wasn't meeting the required standards, he hadn't done too badly as an all-rounder. On the other hand, Surti had excelled in Australia and Queensland took him on board.

What was the need to take such a drastic step, Merchant was asked. It wasn't that Merchant couldn't see their performances. But India's loss in the first Test forced him to change his mind. And he replaced Borde and Surti with Gundappa Viswanath and Eknath Solkar respectively. These players were barely out of their teens.

On his debut in Kanpur, Viswanath was out for a blob. The media tore into Merchant's policy of backing youngsters. However, in the second innings of the same match, Viswanath scored a century. Solkar, too, made his mark as a useful all-rounder and brilliant close-in fielder.

What's all this got to do with Shikhar Dhawan, Rohit Sharma and Ravindra Jadeja, you'd wonder. Well, our selectors have persisted with these youngsters at the cost of two stalwarts, Virender Sehwag and Gautam Gambhir.

One must understand the importance of blooding a youngster at the right time. Such a move requires courage of conviction, and the selection committee must be complimented. Sandeep Patil, Rajinder Singh Hans, Saba Karim, Roger Binny and Vikram Rathour put the country ahead of everyone by taking the drastic step of dropping seniors. You can't simply ignore the worthy players who have been knocking on the doors.

However, no level of assessment is foolproof. In spite of ticking the three boxes of talent, technique and temperament, a newbie could still fail. What happens on the field is a different matter altogether. But selectors are rarely hailed for making a good choice. Success may have many godfathers, but failure has none. Dropping Sehwag and Gambhir and replacing them with Dhawan and Sharma may have backfired.

Dhawan always opened the batting for Delhi but Sharma, one of the most talented batsmen in the country, never faced the new ball even in school. The decision to thrust him into the role was a dangerous one.

After watching Sharma open the batting, oldies recall what happened to Dilip Sardesai. Like Sharma, Sardesai was a connoisseur's delight. Pace or spin, Sardesai's movements were neat and precise. His duels with Erapalli Prasanna were memorable.

A typical No. 4 batsman, Sardesai was mercilessly attacking spinners and was impressive while facing the new ball. While batting in the middle order, he did very well in the 1963-64 series against England. Later, against Australia in 1964, he scored a half-century as an opener.

Appreciating his knack to attack, the selectors asked him to open against the New Zealand attack of Bruce Taylor and Dick Motz in 1965. It wasn't easy handling them, but Sardesai was determined. He ended up scoring an unbeaten double hundred and in the very next Test.

One successful series and the decision was being viewed as a masterstroke. For Sardesai, it was a sort of relief because he no longer had to compete with MAK. Pataudi, Borde and Hanumant Singh in the middle order.

However, amidst all this hype and hoopla, Sardesai's strokes went missing. A natural stroke player, Sardesai had to curb his instincts. And he bottled up game after game; the runs, too, dried up. What followed was a string of failures. And by then, the very selectors who were patting each other on the back, feigned ignorance and dropped him. Ajit Wadekar was asked to choose between Borde and Sardesai for the 1971 West Indies tour. He went with Sardesai. Hailed as the 'Renaissance Man' of Indian cricket, Sardesai was brilliant in the middle order. But in spite of Wadekar's backing, he didn't last long.

Now that Sehwag and Gambhir are no longer the selectors' favourites Sharma is being groomed for the opener's role. However, as we noticed in the case of

Sardesai, you can't just pluck an attacking batsman from the middle order and force him to open.

The selectors never take no for an answer. And given stiff competition in this day and age, sitting out of a match and hoping to make a comeback later is not practical.

That's when a compromise formula makes sense. Sharma could use this chance to open the batting in all forms of the game. To open the batting in limited-overs cricket is one thing; to do the same in Test cricket is a different ballgame altogether. Take the example of Sunil Gavaskar. The great man opened wherever he played. If Sharma agrees to open in Tests, he should open for Mumbai too.

Sardesai and Ashok Mankad grabbed the slots offered to them. Sharma was to make his Test debut a few years ago in Nagpur, but injured himself. He was slated to bat in the middle order then. His journey in ODI cricket hasn't been smooth. It's been a stop-start career. He would certainly like to cement his place in the side. And yes, he badly wants that Test Cap.

When asked about his preparations before opening the innings, Sharma says, "The openers are crucial to any innings because they lay the foundation. Batting in the middle order and opening the innings are different things. I have to change my entire mindset. If the opening pair has a good start, then the middle order batsmen are free to capitalize. Shikhar and I have a good understanding so it makes the flow a lot more natural. I am still learning how to play in this new role assigned to me. I have to be very watchful. I can't lose my wicket too early. Facing the new ball requires a whole new strategy. Given that they use two

new balls in ODIs, things are challenging. But I'm enjoying it. Bowlers have become so intelligent these days that they sort you out even before you realize it. So you've got to be on top of your game mentally and physically."

Sharma is dead right. It's a very difficult job. The legendary Len Hutton opened all his life for Yorkshire and England. When asked to reveal his trade secret, he quipped in his typical Yorkshire accent, "From the non-striker's end". In other words, the best way to tackle the new ball would be to take a single and leave it to the partner.

This is what Sharma will have to learn. If he is keen on opening in Tests, he will have to open the batting in domestic cricket too. Sardesai and Mankad did that willingly. To move up the order is difficult but doable. Ask Joe Root. All you need is the backing of the selectors and, more importantly, your captain. Root batted in the middle order for Yorkshire, because they needed a solid batsman there. But the England selectors were looking for an opener. They had watched him tackle quality fast bowlers with ease, especially at Headingley. They wanted him to do the same for England. Sharma can, and should, do a Root.

If talent is Sharma's middle name, then class is his surname. His malleable wrists and brilliant shots can leave one awestruck. But then again, your abilities can't guarantee you success. Sharma must translate his gifts into some serious performances. He needs to iron out his flaws and work on the mental aspect of his game.

Sharma says Dhoni wants him to open. The skipper's faith in your abilities encourages you to give your best, especially when it's a new job. A natural middle-order batsman, Sharma needed his skipper's backing. And let's give it to Dhoni for showing faith in Sharma and conveying to the selectors that he be given a longer rope. The moment a batsman feels secure, he can do wonders. Look how easily Sharma has made those technical and mental adjustments. It seems he is a natural opener.

Dhawan has attacked bowlers in every domestic tournament one can think of. As an Under-19 player, he displayed a lot of self-belief. And more importantly, his defence was sound.

Unlike most youngsters, Dhawan always had his priorities sorted. He could achieve what he wanted to. "When I was part of the reserves for the Test team, I kept telling myself I'd make a big score on debut. And it happened. I had been visualising this all the time. I worked very hard on my game. I play according to the situation. I like to dominate but as an opener, I have to ensure I play out the new ball. I set some short-term goals, but while chasing it's all about the target. I don't let the pressure get to me."

"But let me be frank", he says, "to face international bowlers who keep bowling at 145-150 kph, you need guts. You have to either rotate the strike or attack whenever a bad ball is bowled. Fast bowlers rarely give you opportunity but when you get one, you must make it count. It's great batting with Rohit. We complement each other. He has a lot of strokes and I love watching him bat. Openers must have a good sense of understanding and I must say we have it."

Another player who belongs to this league of young and promising gentlemen is Ravindra Jadeja. Jadeja, one must say, is unique. If Raj Singh Dungarpur was still around, he would have given Jadeja an honorary life membership of the Cricket Club of India, Mumbai. At an Under-14 camp at the aristocratic club, 30 boys trained under the watchful eyes of Nari Contractor, Hanumant Singh and Vasu Paranjape. Jadeja was the most impressive of the lot. To Dungarpur, he was "a little Salim Durani".

Those four years at the CCI academy did Jadeja a world of good. Be it a net session or a friendly match, the boy would give it all. His recent tussle with Suresh Raina in the West Indies didn't surprise us old-timers. Jadeja was full of energy even in his teens. And he used to get into duels because he wanted his mates to give their best all the time. But not everyone can be a Jadeja!

Contractor recalls those days. "He was supremely talented. He was only 13, but very involved. He turned the ball and also had a good loop. I didn't expect this from a kid. But on batting wickets, he used to bowl a stump-to-stump line. I want to see him succeed in Test cricket," Contractor says.

Jadeja is often compared with Durani. "Both Durani and Jadeja are from Jamnagar. Salim was a bit moody, but he was a brilliant cricketer. He knew a lot of tricks. If Jadeja interacts with him, he will surely gain a lot. Jadeja has quite a few variations up his sleeve. He will only get better. But he needs to bowl longer spells. Jadeja has scored a few triple hundreds in first-class cricket. But have you watched his batting style in ODIs? It seems someone gives him instructions. I think batting at No. 3 for Saurashtra will help him."

Contractor is spot-on. Just like it's difficult to stop the flow of runs in limited-overs cricket, it is an extremely tough task to 'buy' wickets in Test matches. In ODIs, Jadeja chooses to bowl a tight line because his skipper expects him to bowl 10 overs. In five-day cricket, a captain has to have at least three strike bowlers. As the great Erapalli Prasanna says, "Length is mandatory but line is optional." Jadeja has to work on that aspect.

Having been a part of many a crunch game, Jadeja is never overawed. You won't see him lose his cool when a batsman hits him over the top. And as a batsman, he loves to counter-attack. He is a thorough professional. That's why he pulled up Raina for dropping sitters.

Will Jadeja prove to be a good all-rounder in Test cricket? Can he well and truly replace the specialist left arm spinner Pragyan Ojha? Durani has his doubts. "At the moment, Ojha looks comfortable bowling long spells. In Test cricket, a bowler should bowl an attacking line. He must keep dishing out variations. He should be prepared to bowl for two days, without success sometimes. Even though Jadeja hasn't played too much Test cricket, the selectors must try him in the 'A' games. Those four-day matches will show us what he is capable of. The advantage of having Jadeja in the Test team is that he is an all-rounder. And that's not a term you'd associate Ojha with. Our Test team needs all-rounders. During my time, Chandu Borde and Bapu Nadkarni were all-rounders. But if an all-rounder is not genuine, you can't rely on him."

These youngsters have worked very hard to be where they are today. This is what Sharma has to say about dreams and goals. "When you don't realize your dreams, you feel crushed. It's like your world has come crashing down. But I try to stay positive. I keep reminding myself that I need to look at the bigger picture. Cricket has always been my passion. It's my life. I always do what it takes to keep my dream alive. It's not easy to take criticism in your stride, but I use it as a motivational tool. I prefer to let my bat do the talking."

That's the right attitude. The ever-critical media can sometimes get to your nerves. But as a player who's always in the spotlight, Sharma can't afford to lose his cool. He needs to scan the 'advice' he gets and use only what he wants to.

Given that he led the Mumbai Indians to glory in the 2013 IPL, Sharma is being viewed as a future India skipper. At the moment, Virat Kohli is the heir to Dhoni's throne. But make no mistake, Sharma is very much around. This healthy competition between Kohli and Sharma will only help India. Who knows, Dhoni could choose to step down as skipper in one format of the game. The selectors will have to be ready with a healthy bank of prospective captains. If Kohli gets the job, the selectors would still need a back-up. Sharma could be their man.

The manner in which Sharma marshalled his resources during the IPL was brilliant. He came out with a different plan to fox his opponents. And most importantly, the sense of responsibility forced him to bat sensibly. "Being given the responsibility to captain a side like Mumbai Indians is a true honor. Our team had a lot of big names, so it was daunting to captain the side. But I spoke to my teammates, took their opinion and then made my decisions. They always respected that. I enjoy responsibility and it showed in my batting. Captaining a team like this was a great experience. And to be undefeated at home and winning the league was a dream come true. Obviously, captaining India is my ultimate dream. Captaincy made me realize things, I didn't know about myself. I took things in my stride and focused on the solution as opposed to the problem and it had a trickledown effect. I thought I have matured as a cricketer," Sharma says.

Sharma was always a natural striker. He never had to manufacture shots. He was blessed with all the traits of a classy batsman. "My debut for the Mumbai Under-17 side was the turning point of my career. When I got selected, I didn't know whether I would make it to the XI. But I kept sweating it out in the nets and I knew our coach Vasu Paranjape liked my batting."

Even though I didn't make it to the XI in the first league game, I didn't lose heart. I got my chance in the next game and I scored 70-odd. I could see Vasu Sir was extremely happy. He had advised me to play my shots without fear. I went on to score a big hundred in the next game and that knock helped me get into the India Under-17 side. Vasu Sir had faith in my abilities. He kept pushing me to do well and that's how I grew more and more confident," Sharma adds.

All said and done, facing the red ball in England and Australia is no easy task. In India, one can get away with playing away from the body. But on pitches with pace and bounce, one must have a tight defence. It is in this respect that renowned coaches and former international players are apprehensive about Sharma's success as an opener. He has a long way to go.

Contractor, who began his first-class career with a hundred in each innings for Gujarat, says, "It's all a matter of adjustment. I never ever opened for any team till I was forced to open for Gujarat. It so happened that there was a vacancy for an opener, so I had to do the job. Similarly, when Vinoo Mankad didn't turn up for a Test match, I was again forced to open again! Then I realized that the best way to prepare to face the new ball was to open in every match, including a friendly one. And that's what Sharma should do."

Contractor goes on, "At the moment, Sharma plays away from the body. That's because he is a stroke player. If he continues to do that, he won't last long as an opener. On what basis will the selectors pick him as an opener in Test cricket? He is a class player, a superb timer of the ball but he will have to forget his cover drives till he settles in nicely. 'Play straight' should be his mantra."

Dhawan, Sharma and Jadeja bring energy to the Indian team. Young as they are, they still display a different level of maturity. They thrive on pressure and give their best. They reiterate the fact that the good days of Indian cricket are here to stay.

Acknowledgments

No book however small, can be written without the support of family. They create an atmosphere where your mind can think without worries. While writing this book, I was recovering from a high-riskbrain surgery. Though I was clearly instructed by my doctors to not burden my brain post-surgery, I could hardly keep myself detached from the book. When the synopsis of the book was approved by the publishers, I was very motivated. I knew that I should take care of my health but yet could not refrain from engulfing myself in the excitement of this book. I would like to thank the team of doctors who gave me a second life – Dr Paresh Pai, the famous vascular surgeon, Dr Umesh Thakker, Dr Samir Warty, the plastic surgeon and Dr Kirti Dholakia.

I was expected to take a long time to bring my thoughts together due to the surgery. However, my vivid memory did not leave my side even after the surgery. My wife Dr Sandhya had to keep a tab on my workload but did not interfere with my long hours. Having been with me for 35 years, she knew my willpower. She knew that the book strengthened my will more than anything could; it made me stronger every day.

It's true that I slept at night but I would be dreaming of the 60s and 70s; the innings I watched and the golden times I spent with cricketers. Those memories were so fresh that they did not require too much of research. The legends of Indian cricket were in me, ingrained like my very soul, so how could I find them anywhere else? The difficult task that lay ahead of me was to share the stories of the legends I have witnessed, with my readers. I must say that Greg Chappell and Mike Brearley were very helpful with their observations.

My heartfelt thanks to *The Hindu* for allowing quotations from Greg Chappell's articles in this book.

The book has many interesting anecdotes and technical inputs and for that I must thank Greg Chappell, Mike Brearley, Abbas Ali Baig, Salim Durani, Farokh Engineer, Brijesh Patel, Anshuman Gaekwad, Clayton Murzello, Saad Bin Jung (former Hyderabad opener and nephew of Mansur Ali Khan Pataudi) and sports psychologist Dr Rudi Webster of West Indies. I also thank young Shireen Azam who helped me in editing the book and young journalist Derek Abraham in editing the book on behalf of the publishers. How can one forget senior statistician Sudhir Vaidya who provided me vital statistical details of each cricketer.

www.ingramcontent.com/pod-product-compliance
Lightning Source LLC
Chambersburg PA
CBHW062159080426
42734CB00010B/1749